Lonely planet

LONELY PLANET'S

GUIDE TO DEATH,

GRIEF AND REBIRTH

HOW GLOBAL GRIEVING CUSTOMS

CAN HELP US LIVE (AND DIE) WELL

BY ANITA ISALSKA

CONTENTS

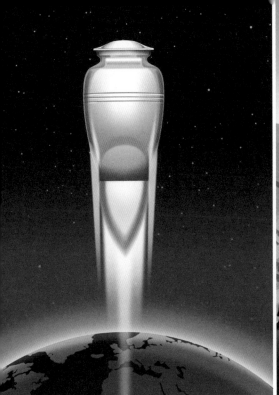

MOURNING

OFFERING

INTRODUCTION

Death is one of the most pervasive themes in art, music and literature, but grief still leaves us lost for words. When someone dies, life's big questions besiege us. We seek solace in mementoes, photographs and rituals of remembrance. Death is universal, and yet every loss is intimate and unique.

In my own family, we have the empty chair. Leaving a spare seat at the table is a common Polish custom, especially on Christmas Eve. My family, descended from World War II transplants to the UK, inherited this tradition – along with pickled herring and Catholic guilt. Some claim the custom grew from pagan beliefs that the dead dine after the living. Others say it's a gesture of that famous Polish hospitality, and a throwback to the Biblical story of Mary and Joseph who couldn't find room at the inn. In the 19th century, empty chairs held space for exiled family members, whose loved ones prayed for their return from forced deportation to Siberia.

Over the years, the empty chair at my family's table also took on a new meaning.

First came the death of my grandmother. A steely and sharp-witted survivor of war, her fierce loyalty and theatrical humour had created a blueprint our entire family would follow. When she died she was no longer the anchor of every social event, but the occupant of our empty chair.

Then came the shocking and sudden death of my uncle; another pillar of our family had fallen. We couldn't build back to how we once were, but we didn't want to forget, either. We made toasts in his words, retold his dry jokes, and looked across at the empty chair – which now felt doubly bare, a monument to repeated loss.

When someone dies, people tell each other: "there are no words". Many of us are on a life-long quest to find them – to grapple with understanding the finality of death and how it impacts how we live.

Death has long been a theme of my own travels: I've pored over inscriptions in Paris' Père-Lachaise Cemetery, contemplated marigold altars on the Day of the Dead (see page 34), and gazed into empty eye-sockets at the bone chapel at Kutná Hora (see page 76). Consciously or subconsciously, I've been trying to wrap myself in wisdom about life and death around the world – to live my own life in a fearless way, and find a better way to navigate loss.

Over the past decade, we've seen this quest reverberate from movies and TV shows. In *Fleabag*, Phoebe Waller-Bridge's contrarian lead character wrestles with guilt after the sudden death of her best friend. In *After Life*, Ricky Gervais plays a small-town newspaper editor living with almost unbearable grief. In both series, death and grief aren't just plot points; they're ever-present companions to the main characters, the source of dark humour and personal growth.

Now, a new movement is emerging to guide people towards expressive, community-oriented ways to grieve. "To heal grief, you need to grieve – and we don't know how to grieve," says Imogen Carn, co-founder of the *Good Mourning* podcast (goodmourning.com.au). "We really need to learn how to

in public about grief and death, so that we can start bringing support, awareness and education into community spaces."

Another podcast breaking the silence is *All There Is*, launched in 2022 by Emmy award-winning broadcast journalist Anderson Cooper. Speaking on the podcast about the isolation he felt after the deaths of his father and brother, Cooper recalled: "I felt like I couldn't speak the same language as other people." Cooper was able to move forward in his grief by bearing witness to the experiences of others: "I went to places where the language of loss was spoken, and the pain that I was feeling inside was matched by the pain all around me. And that's how I learned how to survive."

That search for the languages of loss is also why this book came into being. How do people around the world navigate death and live with grief? And what can these different beliefs and rituals teach us about how to live our lives?

Though the traditions in this book are radically different, certain themes emerge: like creating the space to deeply mourn our loved ones (see page 120) while also celebrating their lives (see page 10). Even the ways we commemorate the dead and remember their lives are astonishingly varied,

express our pain in a safe way, in a way that isn't judged."

Imogen Carn and Sally Douglas launched *Good Mourning* after experiencing first-hand the complexity of grief and the lack of relatable grief resources. "We thought, why don't we start grieving publicly, and letting other people know that all of these

thoughts and feelings are actually normal?" explains Carn.

In cultures where dying and grief occur privately, in hospices, hospitals and the home, the lack of community support can make grief debilitating. "There isn't really strong aftercare support," says Sally Douglas. "What we're trying to do is have conversations so we covered everything from fantasy coffins (see page 86) to extraterrestrial burials (see page 106). Amid the profound reflections and deep sorrows, there's practical guidance, too: like death cleaning (see page 188) and working with an end-of-life doula (see page 184).

Grief is colossal and all-encompassing, but it also challenges us to be humble. We can find relief by placing our personal sorrows in the context of humankind's grand, unfolding drama. People alleviate their pain by returning loved ones to nature, perhaps in a green cemetery (see page 196) or even through a 'sky burial' (see page 218). Through a Buddhist lens (see page 192), death is a transition period, not the final curtain.

Within these pages, we hope you will find symbols, rituals and ways of thinking that resonate with you – not only as you contemplate death, grief and the great beyond, but as inspiration to live life fully.

Anita Isalska, 2024

Previous page: an altar in Janitzio, Michoacan, Mexico during the Day of the Dead. Left top: Sedlec ossuary in Kutná Hora. Left bottom: Celtic Samhain festival celebrated in Glastonbury, England, when it was believed that spirits of the dead can pass into the world of the living. Right: Swayambhunath stupa in Kathmandu, Nepal. Next page: Père-Lachaise Cemetery in Paris, France

CELEBRATING

People celebrate **THE DEAD** IN A startling array OF WAYS, FROM MASS COMMEMORATIONS TO ALL-OUT PARTIES.

THE IRISH WAKE

Irish wakes create a refuge where emotions – and whiskey – can flow. Throughout the night, plaintive songs and raucous games provide catharsis for a community united in grief.

Shut the curtains, cover the mirrors and stop all the clocks: all sense of time and place is suspended at Irish wakes. The home becomes a sanctuary where the whole spectrum of human emotions can be expressed – right by the departed's body.

Before a wake, the body is washed and dressed, and laid on a table or in an open casket in the home. Bereaved family members watch over the body throughout the night, while visiting mourners arrive for music, games and generous glugs of whiskey.

ANCIENT SUPERSTITIONS

Though the majority of Irish households are Christian, wakes long predate Christianity, and many wake customs are steeped in ancient superstition.

A window is opened to allow the deceased's spirit to leave; later, it's closed to prevent the spirit from returning. Some families take pains not to walk between the body and the window, lest they prevent the spirit from departing. Most importantly, the body is never left unattended; children might play beside it, while adults regale memories and in-jokes.

Keening singers (page 123), who lead the community in mourning, are considered to be the human counterparts to banshees, cloaked female spirits who are said to cry and sing when a death is approaching. In Irish folklore, banshees are seen as eerie guardian angels who may follow a

EMBRACING GRIEF'S CONTRADICTIONS

There's no single way to grieve. But mourners often feel pressure to be strong or composed, or inhibited by taboos surrounding death. At an Irish wake, there are no such constraints. With games, pranks and splashes of whiskey, wakes allow one heck of a sendoff, while making space for all emotions to be expressed.

Mourners can tell saucy jokes. They are encouraged to use dark humour, and may be guided by professional mourning singers to let out screams of grief. All of these activities give voice to the intense, and often contradictory, emotions that accompany great loss.

By cultivating a safe, private space for families and friends to gather in grief, wakes create a celebration of humanity right on death's threshold. These shared experiences knit a community together – not just in sorrow, but in humour – and almost defy the finality of death.

particular family and even warn of danger with their harrowing cries.

PLAYING 'WAKE GAMES'

The activities at a wake affirm life in a place of death. They allow a community to strengthen its ties during its moments of greatest vulnerability and transition. But the sense of playfulness serves a practical purpose, too: games and jokes keep mourners awake for the vigil.

Mourners often prank one another, or engage in silly or bawdy games, like 'lift the corpse' (not the actual corpse, fortunately, but a mourner playacting on the floor). And, of course, there's food; sandwiches and cakes to fuel the long night of waiting, with shots of Irish whiskey galore.

Above: A 19th-century engraving depicts an evening wake for the wife of an Irish cottager. Opposite: A traditional wake at The Dubliner Irish bar in Washington, DC.

MELODIES OF MOURNING

Music is the most eloquent expression of grief at Irish wakes, particularly songs from the 'keening' tradition (from the Gaelic *caoineadh*, to weep). Traditional keeners use *sean-nós* (old way) singing, a trilling, ornamental style common to Irish vocal music, though these melodies of mourning are much less common today.

In the past, many families hired professional keeners, often midwives, accustomed to the liminal spaces between life and death. They would arrive to wakes intentionally dishevelled, with matted hair and tattered black garb.

Keening songs tell stories with different tones, depending on whether the death is expected or sudden. The regretful (but matter-of-fact) refrain of the popular funeral song, *The Parting Glass*, sings: 'It fell into my lot that I should rise and you should not', crisply capturing fate's cruelty in a single line. Other keening songs directly address the departed, expressing denial and despair. In *The Lament For Miss Mary Bourke*, the singer pleads: 'Wast thou not happy, Mary? Wast thou not young and fair? Then why should the dread spoiler come, my heart's peace to destroy.' Keening songs often culminate with *gol* (throaty laments or wailing), the lead mourner steering the others to a sorrowful crescendo.

NEW ORLEANS JAZZ FUNERALS

When you join the choir eternal, New Orleans will provide the accompaniment. You'll be sent off with dancing, saxophones and hallelujahs — from friends, family and perfect strangers.

The sound of trumpets cuts through the French Quarter's humid air. Their song is joined by the deep, liquid sound of trombones, and a drummer striking out a slow, solemn beat. Then the musicians come into view, along with a languid procession of people wearing dapper bow-ties and smart dresses. That's when you realise this is a New Orleans funeral — and you know that pretty soon, you'd better get your dancing shoes on.

ONE LAST DANCE

Music courses through New Orleans' veins, so why would funerals be any different? And forget meek laments and tender melodies: this is the birthplace of jazz, where musical traditions brought to the US by enslaved West Africans collided with military music imported by European settlers. Waves of migrants from Sicily and Cuba added their own inflections, including Italian-style trumpet melodies and the rhythmic triplet-

pattern tresillo. The resulting musical cocktail, ragtime, evolved into the swaggering, soaring and often bombastic sound that we know as New Orleans jazz — and nowhere does jazz sizzle and swing quite like The Big Easy.

With the end of slavery, Black communities cultivated the distinctive New Orleans sound at the city's Social Aid and Pleasure Clubs. This is where the New Orleans jazz funeral began: card-carrying members were offered a brass-band sendoff.

CELEBRATING LIFE

Some of the most popular readings at funerals implore us not to wallow in sorrow. 'Do not stand by my grave and weep,' opens Mary Elizabeth Frye's famous poem. 'Wear no forced air of solemnity or sorrow,' urge the oft-quoted words of Henry Scott Holland, 'laugh as we always laughed.' The New Orleans funeral is the true embodiment of this sentiment, with shared joy and community strength at the heart of the proceedings.

Grief can be unbearably heavy – but your community can help carry the load. At a jazz funeral, the thunderous sound of brass and drums summon onlookers to join the second line, marching in formation behind grieving friends and relatives. Their role is to amplify the proceedings and give the departed a sendoff with all the pomp and ceremony that they would wish for themselves. The procession becomes a celebration of the departed's life – and of life itself.

JOINING THE SECOND LINE

The procession at a jazz funeral starts with a solemn tone. A parade master, clad smartly in black, leads a procession from the church service and along the streets to the burial ground. This group accompanies the coffin – which may be carried on a horse-drawn hearse – and is made up of the deceased's family, their closest friends and the band (usually a brass band and percussion). They might carry wooden pickets with photos of the deceased on them, and though it's common to wear black, this is New Orleans: there'll be brightly coloured hats, feather boas, pearls, lace and huge umbrellas.

Following behind the main procession is the second line, an essential ingredient in a New

Above: Jazz funeral neon sign on Bourbon Street in New Orleans' French Quarter. Opposite: Musicians play on the street outside the Orpheum Theatre.

Orleans funeral. It's formed of friends and acquaintances, along with passersby and neighbours who hear the fray and rush outside to march, free-form dancing along the way. The origins of second lines can be traced to Gambia and Senegal's traditional dances, where children dance a second circle around a ring of adults. The celebratory dance style is also thought to originate in West Africa, where certain funerary rites involved a celebration of the spirit departing the body and returning to its ancestors.

SWINGING CELEBRATIONS

Jazz funerals undergo a dramatic change in tone, either once the church is out of sight or after

Above: Jazz funeral second lines are thought to be inspired by West African funeral ceremonies, like this one in Cameroon. Opposite: A jazz funeral parade passes Our Lady of Guadalupe Church on Rampart St.

EXPERIENCING A NEW ORLEANS JAZZ FUNERAL

Anyone who witnesses the stage presence of a New Orleans jazz funeral might wonder: how can I get that kind of sendoff myself? After all, who wouldn't want to shuffle off this mortal coil to the dramatic sound of booming tubas and clashing cymbals, while behatted revellers pirouette through the streets in your name?

Technically, anyone can plan a New Orleans jazz funeral, although these days it's usually musicians and prominent local figures who receive this distinction. Unless you live in the city, and are a member of the 70-plus Social Aid and Pleasure Clubs – benevolent organisations founded since the 1800s – this honour doesn't come cheap. The main cost, on top of the usual casket, flowers and reception expenses, is hiring a band and parade master.

If you have the chance to participate in one, come attired in traditional black – but give it a New Orleans twist with bold accessories. Don't forget sunglasses and a parasol, ideally decorated to heighten the effect of twirling it as you strut along in the second line. But it isn't considered disrespectful to show up in streetwear, as long as you enter into the spirit of the proceedings and follow the parade master's cues... there are no mere spectators at a jazz funeral!

the body is buried. The parade master will expertly manipulate the crowd into an upbeat, revelrous mood. The drumbeats stomp faster, the saxophones soar and the dancing turns raucous. Hands clap, handkerchiefs are waved in the air, and the umbrellas that were used to shelter mourners from the sun turn into dancing props, swung in time with the beat. All of a sudden, it's a party.

Hanging around hoping for a funeral isn't a good look. But in a city famous for its ostentatious sendoffs, stranger things have happened: sanctuaries like St Louis Cathedral and St Mary's Church are common starting points, and tourists have been known to join the fray.

TAKING A FINAL BOW

If the dearly departed is a musician, you can bet that New Orleans' jazz royalty will show up for the funeral procession. Rock 'n' roll pianist and musical pioneer Fats Domino had a second-line jazz funeral in 2017, in which a brass band blared his songs.

But no coffin, no problem. Second lines are also a way

of celebrating the memory of well-known people, regardless of whether it's formally their funeral. New Orleans held a second line after the death of *Golden Girls* star and pop-culture icon Betty White, on the day that would have been her 100th birthday. The artist formerly known as Prince was also celebrated in this way, by thousands of purple-clad fans who poured through the streets playing his music on portable stereos.

Most poignantly, multiple jazz funerals have been held in honour of more than 1800 people who died during Hurricane Katrina, both in the aftermath of the disaster and on the 10-year anniversary. The processions featured a horse-drawn hearse with an empty coffin, flanked by firetrucks and a brass band, and allowed a moment of community remembrance. In New Orleans, you dance in defiance of death — and on behalf of those who can dance no more.

Opposite: The wrought iron lace of a French Quarter balcony. Right: Arcade Fire and the Preservation Hall Jazz Band play during a traditional jazz funeral for David Bowie in 2016.

NO-EXPENSE-SPARED CHINESE FUNERALS

Chinese funerals rival lavish wedding ceremonies when it comes to pomp and ritual. From Hong Kong to Taiwan, Buddhists, Confucians and Taoists have mastered the art of staging a grand exit.

People often daydream about who would come to their funeral. Friends and family? Close colleagues? Perhaps the odd former girlfriend or boyfriend? In China, the whole neighbourhood gets involved – a low-key service with only the closest family members is simply not the done thing.

In many Chinese communities, funerals are as much about what you show as who you know. Status has played an integral role in Chinese society since at least the Qin Dynasty (221–206 BCE), when the populace was formally stratified into nobles, farmers and peasants, artisans and craftspeople, and merchants.

The funerals of highfliers can cost millions of yuan, coming complete with explosive firework displays, gold-plated coffins, jade burial urns and lorry loads of Chunghwa cigarettes and premium Moutai Baijiu rice wine for mourners. Nothing says you've done well in life quite like a lavish sendoff.

DEATH WITH STATUS

Chinese funerals typically begin with a personal wake held for family and friends that lasts up to seven days and includes rituals focused on warding off evil spirits and preparing the deceased for the afterlife.

The whole community often joins in for the final procession to the burial or cremation site. The ceremony includes loud music to scare away evil forces and a sumptuous banquet laid on for attending mourners.

GRIEVING, SHARED

A gilded coffin won't be to everyone's taste, but other aspects of Chinese funerals have a broader application. The merits of being allowed to grieve loudly and publicly may resonate with anyone who has grown up in a society where grief is treated as something to be seen but not heard.

With a mourning period lasting anything from 49 days to three years, China's formalised grieving schedule might seem strange to people more used to private mourning, but it gives structure to a process that may otherwise be overwhelming. Rituals such as tomb-sweeping preserve the relationship with the deceased, making the gravesite a place of comfort.

Local community involvement in funeral rituals reassures families that their relatives were valued in life, and honoured with the appropriate filial piety in death. Think of it as socialised mourning – a notable counterpoint to Western traditions of suffering in silence.

Despite attempts by the authorities to crack down on extravagant funerals, ceremonies for public figures can attract tremendous outpourings of public grief. The 2021 funeral of Chinese national hero Yuan Longping – hailed as the 'father of hybrid rice' – drew some 100,000 mourners to Changsha in Hunan Province.

"The involvement of the local community helps a great deal with grief, because it is built on – and strengthens – the sense of the interdependence of people in the community," explains Hongbing Yu, Assistant Professor of Culture and Semiotics at Toronto Metropolitan University.

This sense of togetherness can transcend social boundaries. In 2010, the funeral of Taiwanese gangster Lee Chao-hsiung in Taichung City attracted 20,000 well-wishers, including members of the Bamboo Union, Four Seas Triad and Celestial Way gangs, local police, mayors and politicians – even the speaker of the Taiwanese parliament.

ADMIRATION FOR THE ANCESTORS

However, even the most outrageous ceremonies are only partly about social standing. For relatives, the primary motivation is filial piety – a codified system of moral obligations towards one's parents and ancestors, laid down by the philosopher Confucius in the 6th century BCE.

Above: A man sets up offerings at a deceased relative's columbarium in Chai Wan Cemetery, Hong Kong. Opposite: Primary school students paint red on the tombstone of an unknown martyr at the Red Army Martyrs' Cemetery in Sichuan province on Tomb-Sweeping Day.

CASH TO BURN

Even at the most modest Chinese funeral service, you'll find people burning through money. To ensure that relatives are comfortable in the next life, huge bundles of ceremonial banknotes – known as 'spirit money', 'hell money' or 'joss paper' – are burned in censers or placed in the coffin, transferring wealth to loved ones in the spirit world.

These ceremonial banknotes feature images of the Jade Emperor (the ruler of heaven) or King Yan (the monarch of hell), to be used as gifts or bribes in the next life – but joss paper isn't limited to mock money. At Chinese funerary stores you'll find paper dresses, paper shoes, paper cigarettes and lighters, paper Rolexes, paper iPhones, paper cars, paper houses...

Other traditions, however, are undeniably about status in this life. In Taiwan, the funeral processions of successful men are often accompanied by so-called funeral strippers – dancers who perform mildly risqué routines around the coffin. As well as being a symbol of wealth, these stand-in mourners draw additional crowds to the funeral, ensuring a prestigious arrival into the afterlife.

"Filial piety is important because it has the power of consolidating the bonds between parents and children as well as the sense of their interdependence," says Hongbing Yu. "One of the most common ways for children to demonstrate filial piety at funerals is through expressive displays of grief."

Allowing a parent to pass on to the next life without a public outpouring of emotion would be a shameful dereliction of duty. Kusang vocal laments are a common part of the process, and professional female mourners, known as *kusangpo*, are sometimes hired to add extra volume.

Filial duties don't end with the funeral service. Children maintain a lifelong relationship with their parents' tombs through designated rituals on red-letter days, such as Qingming – the spring Tomb-Sweeping Festival – when family members clean the graves of their parents and make offerings to past generations.

To accommodate this tradition, some Chinese communities have elevated tombs to the level of part-time homes for the living. In the Chinese Cemetery in Manila, you'll find graves that almost qualify as luxury apartments, complete with crystal chandeliers, stained-glass windows, kitchenettes, working bathrooms and air-conditioning.

Above: Joss paper money is set alight to send off the deceased. Opposite: A shop in Kowloon, Hong Kong, stocked with paper funeral offerings.

© MISELY | SHUTTERSTOCK

DEDICATED DAYS FOR THE DEAD

The Tomb-Sweeping Festival of Qingming is just the most well-known of a string of Chinese festivals that focus on honouring the ancestors. During the Hungry Ghost Festival (page 61) – known as Zhongyuan in Taoism and Yulanpen in Buddhism – the deceased are believed to be released from the lower realms and able to enter the land of the living, who can take steps to alleviate their suffering by making offerings of food, and burning incense and joss paper.

The deceased are also the focus during Chongyang (or Chung Yeung) – the Double Ninth Festival – when families sip drinks infused with chrysanthemum and lay on feasts of suckling pig and fruit for the dead, which are finished off by relatives once the spirits have had their fill. It's all part of a festival calendar devoted to keeping the dead alive, in a society in which leaving the graves of parents untended is the ultimate taboo.

Close to temples and cemeteries, you'll find Chinese religious shops doing a brisk trade in joss paper in preparation for these ceremonies. Queen's Rd West in Hong Kong's Sai Wan district is famous for stores specialising in representations of contemporary items, such as air-conditioners, racetracks and even Viagra tablets.

GAI JATRA'S MERRY PASSAGE OF SOULS

Every year in Nepal's Kathmandu Valley, a bell-ringing parade of stately cows and colourfully dressed people ushers the dead into their next life – dancing and jesting along the way.

The clamour of drums and trumpets grows louder. A long procession is snaking through the city of Bhaktapur, past towering statues and triple-roofed temples. People are leading cows through the shop-lined streets, while dancers in crimson masks and shaggy wigs leap from side to side. Some members of the procession are holding aloft portraits of family members, with ribbons and marigold wreaths swinging from the picture frames. Meanwhile, children with curly moustaches drawn on their faces gawp, wide-eyed at the spectacle.

In Bhaktapur, as in many other cities in Nepal's Kathmandu Valley, August or September bring a grand *jatra* (street carnival) of joy and remembrance. This is Gai Jatra, a festival of spiritual renewal that takes place each year when the dead are guided out of this life to ringing sounds of games, music and laughter.

LAUGHING THROUGH GRIEF

Gai Jatra takes place on the one day each year when souls can pass on to the realm of the dead and be freed from the cycle of death and rebirth. On this auspicious day, when the membrane between life and death is most porous, there is mischief in the air. People attending Gai Jatra rejoice in jokes and satire; not only do they dress up in costumes and draw moustaches on their children's

UNITED IN GRIEF

The festival of Gai Jatra commemorates the dead and eases their passage out of this life, but it's also an emotional release for those who are left behind. Through humour, costumes and music, families find ways to experience joy while they remember the loved ones they have lost.

The concept of joy's healing power dates back to the festival's origins. According to legend, townspeople weren't just helping their grieving queen crack a smile; by coming out in droves, they were reminding her that she wasn't alone in grief.

Today's Gai Jatra processions, where community members display photographs of dead family members, embed a feeling of solidarity among the grieving. Whether it's an annual event, a support group or a place of remembrance (a monument or cemetery), being present with others who are experiencing loss can be a powerful way to reduce the loneliness of grieving.

faces, they cross-dress, do impressions and mock politicians and public figures.

Humour and good cheer are at the origins of Gai Jatra. The festival began under King Pratap Malla, who ruled the medieval kingdom of Kantipur in the Kathmandu Valley in the 17th century. After the death of his teenage son from smallpox, the king urged his subjects to revive the queen from her deep grief – and a succession of cows, jesters and outlandishly dressed locals rose to the challenge of making her smile. Ever since, Gai Jatra has been an annual occasion where a merry human-bovine parade pours through the streets of Nepalese towns, rousing cheer while remembering the dead.

Above: Crowds flock to the Gai Jatra festival. Opposite top: Blessing the photograph of a deceased family member. Middle: Bhaktapur youth dance in traditional dress during the procession. Bottom: Women parade in Kathmandu.

SACRED COWS & SPIRITUAL CHARIOTS

In Hinduism, cows are considered sacred symbols of motherhood and prosperity, so these gentle beasts are the most distinguished guests at Gai Jatra. Anyone who has had a family member die during the preceding year will lead a cow during the procession. However, it's very common to use a symbolic stand-in, such as a person wearing a cow mask or face-paint. There will also be bamboo effigies of cows to get the bovine numbers up.

Cow masks and makeup aside, people also don colourful clothing for Gai Jatra: women might wear richly embroidered Gunyo-Cholo (sari-blouse sets) and men their finest Daura-Suruwal (the national costume of tunics and pants). Children are clad in garments that trail on the ground, connecting earth and air and symbolising how the dead must pass between the two.

The city of Bhaktapur hosts some of the most flamboyant celebrations, where attendees pull Taha-Macha (ornate bamboo chariots), in an eight-day parade. Each chariot bears a photo of a dearly departed person, so families can symbolically usher their loved ones into the next life.

MEXICO'S DÍA DE MUERTOS

With its skulls and flower-framed altars, Mexico has the world's most famous festival of remembrance. But beyond Día de Muertos, an extraordinary death culture permeates Mexican art, literature and everyday life.

Whether or not you have experienced Día de Muertos, Mexico's annual Day of the Dead, maybe you can picture the scene. There are women in floral dresses, their faces painted with elaborate skull designs. They clasp glowing candles as they walk from altar to altar, where people have laid bright marigolds and photographs of their dead loved ones. Children are nibbling *panes de muerto* (pastries decorated with sugary bones), while music and the sweet musk of burning sage float on the breeze.

The poet Octavio Paz described the typical Mexican person as 'familiar with death, jokes about it, caresses it, sleeps with it, celebrates with it'. Día de Muertos is the most famous example of that mindset, but the festival is just one window into Mexico's flourishing death culture.

BETWEEN MYTH & REALITY

Día de Muertos has captured the world's imagination so strongly that its symbols can be found gracing everything from T-shirts to fast-food menus. The festival is subject to projection and myth-making by other cultures — and sometimes new narratives are imported right back to Mexico.

The 2015 James Bond movie *Spectre* begins with an eye-popping Day of the Dead parade in Mexico City, complete with gigantic skeleton floats, wreaths of marigolds and crowds of women in skeleton face-paint. There's just one snag: until the

KEEPING DEATH CLOSE

In Frida Kahlo's mesmerising self-portrait *Thinking about Death*, the artist paints herself with a tiny skull in the middle of her forehead. But although death is at the (literal) forefront of Kahlo's mind, she depicts herself against a backdrop of flourishing greenery. It isn't a portrayal of life *defiant* against death; it's life made more precious and beautiful because of death. The painting perfectly encapsulates Mexico's death culture: to live fully, you must embrace death. By doing so, you will be able to fully appreciate life's urgency and potential.

The joy and humour with which Mexican people remember their dead is an impetus for how they live their lives. The knowledge that we and our loved ones will die highlights life's transience, thereby encouraging us to seize opportunities and seek joy. By embracing death, rather than fearing it or trying to contain it, death becomes an accompaniment to a life well lived.

movie was released, Mexico City had never held such a parade. But nowadays, a large-scale parade is hosted here every year.

BRINGING JOY TO THE DEAD

In its simplest form, Día de Muertos involves family and community remembrance at home and in cemeteries. On and around 1 November each year, people visit graves and lovingly assemble home *ofrendas* (altars). Each altar is colourfully customised to the tastes of the dead: draped in fine embroidery, ornamented with skull figurines, illuminated by candlelight, and almost always framed by orange marigold flowers. Families and friends lay treasured photographs on the altars, along with anything the deceased enjoyed in life: cigars, books, their favourite

Above: Banners fly at Parroquia De San Miguel Arcángel Church in Guanajuato. Opposite: Commemorations glow and decorations adorn the country on Día de Muertos.

candy. It's a way to honour and delight the dead, as well as a reminder that we too will die.

In some communities, entire streets are lined with altars. For families, they're a focal point of remembrance. But members of the community also visit altars to people they never knew in life, 'meeting' them for the first time postmortem.

LA CATRINA: MEXICO'S DAME OF THE DEAD

These celebrations hark back to Mexico's indigenous Olmec, Maya, and Aztec peoples. Pre-Hispanic people would leave offerings to guide their ancestors' journeys through nine levels of the underworld, a precursor to the fruit-laden altars of today's Día de Muertos festivities. After

Above: The Día de Muertos parade in Mexico City, inspired by James Bond. Opposite: The festival is celebrated with colourful costumes and skeleton face masks in San Antonio, Texas.

SEE IT FOR YOURSELF

Despite James Bond movies taking liberties with the truth, Día de Muertos parades aren't just Hollywood fabrication – and you can experience the most renowned festivities in Oaxaca and Michoacán. In Oaxaca, people light candles and decorate altars around the Panteón General, and there are stalls where you can peruse traditional arts and crafts. Meanwhile in Michoacán, you'll see people attired with flowers and skulls, and cemeteries aglow with candles and bright marigold wreaths. One highlight is the candlelit parade of boats around Isla Janitzio. (And yes, the relatively new annual parade in Mexico City is popular, too.)

Day of the Dead activities can also be seen anywhere with a thriving Mexican population. Los Angeles has one of the biggest Mexican communities in the US, and the processions along Olvera St, performances at the Hollywood Forever Cemetery and community altars offer high-octane and intimate ways to encounter Mexican death culture. San Francisco's Mission District is another Californian hub for Day of the Dead activity, with a procession and community altars in Potrero del Sol Park. Over in San Antonio, Texas, you can watch the parade along the River Walk, then contemplate your mortality over a plate of tamales.

Catrina, complete with bonnets, floral dresses and makeup that contours their faces into skulls. They might even be accompanied by a dandyish male counterpart, with skull face-paint and a top hat. There's no more powerful way to confront death than becoming a walking, talking memento mori.

BLESSED BLOOMS

The significance of *cempasúchil* (marigolds) also originates in Aztec legend, in a story about two lovers, Xóchitl and Huitzilin. When Huitzilin died in battle, Xóchitl beseeched the sun god to reunite her with her dead lover. Unwilling to reverse the finality of death, the god transformed Xóchitl into a marigold, and allowed Huitzilin to be reborn as a hummingbird who could visit the flower.

Ever since, marigolds have symbolised the hope of reunion after death. Not only do their fiery colours illuminate almost every altar, their fragrance – which drew the hummingbird Huitzilin back to his lover – is thought to connect the living and the dead. When this scent hangs thick in the air at Día de Muertos celebrations, it has the power to rouse immense nostalgia and hope.

Spanish conquest in the 16th century, these ancient rites became interwoven with newly arrived Catholic traditions.

Mexico's original lady of the dead is Mictēcacihuātl, an ancient goddess who helps guide the dead. Nowadays death takes the form of La Catrina, a flower-crowned skeleton who is Día de Muertos' most famous symbol. La Catrina became legendary in 1910, when the Mexican illustrator José Guadalupe Posada sketched a satirical image of a skeleton wearing a flower-laden hat. This was a biting mockery of high-society Mexicans imitating European fashions and discarding their own Mexican culture. It's ironic, then, that many cultures have adopted and appropriated La Catrina – who was originally created to ridicule artifice and warn of cultural dilution.

Attend Día de Muertos celebrations and you're sure to see women styled as La

Above and opposite: The *ofrenda*, or altar, is a key element of Día de Muertos commemorations.

FAMILY REUNITED AT THE *OFRENDA*

Regina Campos Reyes grew up in Aguascalientes, Mexico. She and her family run Lolo Mercadito, an online store promoting Mexican culture.

The last week of October, my mom would take us to the *mercado* to get the essentials for the *ofrenda*. What I looked forward to the most were the *calaveritas* (sugar skulls) that had a string from the top connecting the jaw which would open, so it looked like it could talk.

We had a special corner in our house for the *ofrenda*. Decorating it was my favourite part, and today I understand why – it felt like a family reunion. My mom would place pictures of my family one by one at the *ofrenda*. Each photo would be accompanied by an explanation of who they were. Not their lineage or relation to me, but a detailed real-life description of how my mother thought of them, with their personalities, flaws, and anecdotes to prove what she meant.

I learned that *mi abuela* loved her cats and dogs, so we would put treats and food out for them as they would, obviously, be accompanying her. Then *mi abuelito* would appear, but he had to be apart from *mi abuela* because he didn't like cats – but we had to make sure to add a radio so he could listen to the news and sports. *Mi tío* Enrique would go in the centre because we knew he could keep the peace between them all with his joyful spirit.

I knew their favourite drinks: Coca Cola for all *mis abuelitos* and a Pacífico beer for *mi tío*. I learned about the mistakes they made and the ones they did not. I learned of their strength, but more importantly, I learned of their love.

I remember being scared some nights by the idea of ghosts visiting my house. But this fear went away as soon as my mom explained: these were not ghosts, but *mi familia*, who loved me with all their heart and wanted nothing but for me to be happy. I know where I come from, and I got to meet my ancestors through the eyes of my mom.

TURNING THE BONES IN MADAGASCAR

Every few years, Malagasy people throw a party so epic that even the dead are invited. This is the Turning of the Bones, where bodies are exhumed while loved ones dance and feast.

Dancing with the dead might sound like an image borrowed from a medieval tapestry. But when Malagasy people bring the dead out of their tombs for Famadihana (the Turning of the Bones), the atmosphere is celebratory and exuberant. Famadihana isn't a time for tears – it's a time for remembrance, joyful celebration, and to show care for the dead.

To many Malagasy people, the transition between human life and the next life isn't instantaneous. When a person's physical signs of life cease, they enter a liminal state. They're no longer active participants in the world of the living, but they don't cross over to the realm of the dead until their physical body has fully decomposed. The Turning of the Bones is also an opportunity to win favour: the dead are believed to be conduits between God and the living, with the power to influence events on Earth.

MESSAGES FROM BEYOND

The Turning of the Bones takes place every five to seven years, but the exact date requires a supernatural RSVP. First, someone in the deceased's family will experience a prophetic dream in which an ancestor complains of the cold. Next, an astrologer is consulted to advise on the most auspicious time to open the family tomb. Timing is critical to ensure the dead aren't offended or disturbed.

THE DEAD WALK AMONG US

For cultures that consider dead bodies to be taboo or contaminating (both physically and spiritually), the Turning of the Bones might sound confronting or visceral. But this festival makes a spiritual truth tangible: the dead never really leave us.

When we are newly bereaved, we experience a painful cognitive dissonance when attempting to re-categorise our loved ones as 'dead' and no longer part of our world. After all, our minds still swim with memories of passed relatives and friends as they were during life. We may even be surrounded by mementoes that remind us of their personality and physical presence.

The Turning of the Bones gives bereaved people a break from that painful status quo: their loved ones are no longer alive, but they can be considered temporary visitors back to the world of the living. The natural instinct to communicate with, and care for, the dead can find expression and relief.

Once the perfect date is decided, word goes out and family members will travel from far and wide. Even the dead are given advance notice of the upcoming festivities.

FAMILY REUNION ACROSS DEATH'S THRESHOLD

The build-up to the Turning of the Bones is hotly anticipated, and the ritual is a considerable investment. Not only are there new silk shrouds to purchase for the dead and tomb upkeep to think about, there's a whopping feast of food and rum to prepare for guests. There might be days of negotiation to decide on the proceedings — and the expenses associated with hosting guests.

When the tomb is opened, family members busy themselves unwrapping the shrouded bodies, cleaning them and re-clothing them in white silk burial shrouds — sometimes tucking a small gift that they would have enjoyed in life into the folds. The names of the dead are written on these pristine new shrouds, and they are spritzed with perfume.

GOOD LUCK FROM THE DEAD

Old shrouds are thought to be infused with otherworldly powers, so they aren't discarded. They're kept for good luck, especially by women trying to conceive children, who place

Above: A communal feast is part of the festivities. Opposite: Villagers dance and chant while carrying the shrouded remains of their departed family members back to the tomb.

Above: Guests play music while waiting for the family tomb to open. Opposite: Elaborate tombs at the Rova (Royal Palace) of Antananarivo.

tomb feetfirst, which is believed to have a spiritually transforming effect; then it is returned to the tomb headfirst, to represent that the person now dwells in the world of ancestors.

AN ANCIENT ISLAND CUSTOM

The Famadihana tradition isn't entirely unique: it has parallels in parts of Southeast Asia, such as in Sulawesi, Indonesia. Here, the Torajan people treat the recently deceased as though they are in a twilight state, symbolically feeding them, speaking to them and even parading them around the village during the annual Ma'Nene festival (page 96).

In Madagascar, the Turning of the Bones is thought to have begun in the 17th century, but a lack of historical records has obscured its origins. The Catholic Church once objected to this practice, but has since held its tongue about whether ancestor worship conflicts with Christian teachings. Still, commitment to this remembrance tradition has dwindled because of generational preferences, as well as the expense. Fears about public health also threaten Famadihana: the ritual has sometimes been blamed for outbreaks of pneumonic plague, though many scientists say that the length of time between each Turning of the Bones makes transmission from infected bodies unlikely.

them beneath their beds. It's also common for vessels of water to be sealed up in tombs and retrieved during the Turning of the Bones, and then sprayed around the home for good luck.

Bodies may be removed from their tombs on multiple Famadihanas, but the first time is done with particular care. The body must be removed from the

DRESSED FOR A FINAL DANCE

Once wrapped in their new silks, the dead are ready to join the party. Living guests lovingly caress the shrouded bodies, catch them up on family news, and consult them about their problems. They even hold the dead aloft and dance to the music of drums, trumpets and traditional *sodina* flutes.

But once daylight dims, fear of night's sinister powers draws the festival to an end. The community replace the dead upside-down in their tombs and reseal them, already looking forward to next year when they'll see them again.

MADAGASCAR'S COLOURFUL TOMBS

Instead of a cemetery, many villages in Madagascar have a 'city of the dead' made up of intricate 'house tombs'. Families save for years to afford one of these tombs, which can cost the equivalent of several thousand dollars – which is an astonishing sum in a country that consistently ranks among the world's poorest. The tomb is often more extravagant than the family home.

Made of stone, concrete or brick, the tombs house generations of a family's dead, or even the dead from multiple families, and are remarkably decorative both inside and out. They are usually surrounded by a fence or low wall and flanked by protective symbols like zebu horns, which represent power and wealth, or *aloalos* (funerary poles) with sculptures evoking the deceased's life.

Tombs are splashed with bright colours, ornamented with tiles and decorated with geometric patterns. They might be adorned with symbols that represent the transition or journey to the afterlife, like boats and doorways; or Madagascar's flora and fauna. It's common to see paintings depicting dead family members holding objects symbolic to the family, or even sewing, riding a horse or playing the guitar – cheerful reminders of who they were in life.

NIGERIA'S SECOND BURIALS

It takes more than one funeral to pass from this life to the next. That's why Nigerian families hold second burials, complete with costumes, pageantry and uproarious drumming.

The funeral procession moves to the sound of trumpets and frenetic drumming. Women dressed in black-and-white *ukara* cloth wail, while suited pallbearers bop and sway as they carry the coffin. Nigerian people spare no expense when giving loved ones a stately sendoff – and they'll do it all again, on an even grander scale, in a few months' time.

Many Nigerian families hold not only a funeral but a separate celebration of the dead: (*ikwa ozu*), often referred to as a 'second burial'. Even more lavish than the literal burial, these celebratory ceremonies guarantee that the deceased will pass on to their posthumous role: becoming an ancestor.

FUNERAL CUSTOMS GALORE

With over 250 tribes, twice that number of languages and a kaleidoscope of regional differences, Nigeria's end-of-life traditions form a rich tapestry.

Traditional tribal beliefs are interlaced with Christianity and Islam, against a backdrop of taboos around death – many of which are now being eclipsed by religion or modern sensibilities. For example, one old tradition urges widows to drink the water used to wash their husband's corpse, to prove they weren't responsible for his death – a superstition that modern Nigerians are challenging.

STRIKING THE BALANCE

Many grieving families face a dilemma: how to choose funeral rituals that honour both ancestral customs and the family's evolving belief systems? In Nigeria, many Igbo people find a middle ground by holding a Christian funeral ceremony as well as a second burial. While intermingling different customs can seem like a compromise, this satisfies mourners of differing belief systems (and covers all bases to ensure the deceased passes on to the next life).

Second burials also allow mourners to strike a balance between the emotional and practical necessities that accompany a death. It might be necessary to bury a body soon after death, but that doesn't mean you're emotionally (or financially) prepared to give them the sendoff they deserve. By holding a second burial – with a memorial or celebration on a later date, or anniversary – friends and family can gather again to mourn and remember long after the funeral.

But one belief remains steadfast across ethnic groups: reverence for ancestors. And Nigeria's three largest Indigenous tribes – the Hausa-Fulani, the Igbo and the Yoruba – all honour their forebears in different ways.

The Hausa-Fulani people, Nigeria's largest ethnic group, mostly follow Islamic burial customs (page 127), including ritual cleansing, simple burial and orientation of the body toward Mecca. However, beliefs in restless spirits still linger, meaning some Hausa prayers invoke ancestors to keep them

Above and opposite: Drummers and performers dressed as spirits of the dead take part in the Eyo Festival, a masquerade that takes over Lagos Island when a notable person dies.

appeased. Meanwhile the Yoruba people, more than 20% of Nigeria's population, believe in reincarnation within families. For the Yoruba, easing the departure of a family member's spirit is essential to ensure its rebirth within the same family line.

Yoruba people also hold second burials, but it's the Igbo people, Nigeria's third-largest ethnic group, who are most closely associated with this custom. To the Igbo, death is the passage from life to a new role as an ancestor, and only *ikwa*

ozu – a second burial – can ensure this vital transition.

COMING HOME FOR BURIAL
A funeral typically takes place at the deceased's ancestral village or, for women, their husband's village. The body is readied for its homecoming journey with a daubing of scarlet camwood dye. When it arrives, family members gather for a vigil, with traditional music and speeches.

Here's where it gets expensive: funerals mean buying new clothing (family members often coordinate to

wear the same pattern, and are unlikely to wear these outfits again), as well as livestock to slaughter, and enough alcohol to quench the thirst of dozens of attendees. Like in Ghana (page 87), it's common to hire dancing pallbearers to jive and shimmy the coffin to its final resting place. But the emotional temperature of the proceedings will vary: if the deceased led a long and prosperous life and is survived by offspring, the mood will be mournful but celebratory. The funeral of a person who died a sudden or untimely death will be much more muted.

Meanwhile, the family's eldest daughter has a special job: the *ino uno akwa* rite. She's responsible for the deceased being nourished in the afterlife, and to do so she must eat their favourite meals in silence from dawn until dusk.

THE SECOND BURIAL

The literal burial takes place during the funeral. The body is lowered into the ground and mourners throw sand or earth into the grave. But the second burial can be up to a year after death – allowing families time to save up enough money for days, even weeks, of festivities.

With colourful costumes, masks and ceremonial exchanges, performance is at the heart of second burials. Family elders will pointedly question descendants about their preparedness for the funeral proceedings, to ensure the deceased moves on to ancestor status without a hitch. There's usually a mock-trial to uncover who is responsible for the death, even if it isn't attributable to anything other than old age or disease. Men might don wooden Mmanwu (spirit of the dead) masks to invoke ancestors and act out ancient morality tales.

Not only does the second burial ensure the deceased assumes ancestor status, it protects family members from being assailed by evil spirits for neglecting their ceremonial duties. Above all, it reinforces the belief that death isn't a separation, but a redefinition of family relationships. The second burial sets up a new and enduring family dynamic, where loving bonds remain strong even after death.

Left: Pallbearers and musicians at a 'first' funeral in a Nigerian village.

FESTIVAL OF THE SPIRITS

Masked performances are common at Nigerian funerals, but one Yoruba festival takes them to a whole new level of drama. The Eyo Festival began in the late 19th century as a way to mark the death of an Oba (chief or king). Even today, when a person of great repute dies (or on a ceremonial occasion like a new Oba being installed), this impressive masquerade pours through the streets of Lagos Island.

Performers dress as Agogoro Eyo, the spirits of the dead: they're cloaked head to toe in white cloth that billows dramatically as they dance. Each wears a wide-brimmed hat, decorated with colours and symbols connected to their ancestry, and wields an Opambata (palm branch, each one with unique decorations).

With their ceremonial weapons and veiled faces, the performers resemble a righteous army of otherworldly beings. They brandish their staffs to greet festival attendees and chase away prohibited clothing or items (caps and cloth head-coverings aren't allowed, nor can people smoke or ride motorcycle taxis into the festival). As they dance, people sing and clap to the rhythm of snares and ceremonial Gbedu drums. It's a suitably grandiose way to usher a Lagos legend into their next life.

DEAD CAN DANCE
Festivals & Celebrations of Death

Around the world, people venerate and celebrate the dead in a startling array of ways, from mass commemorations to all-out parties.

Festivals to honour and worship ancestors are as varied as the world's cultures, from Mexico's colourful Día de Muertos (page 35) to the jokes and jollity of Gai Jatra in Nepal (page 31) or Sulawesi's Ma'Nene festival (page 96), in which departed loved ones are ritually exhumed to take part in the fun. In traditions of mass ancestor worship, whole communities come together to pay their respects, make offerings and even place a down-payment on their own successful departure from this life.

In Japan, India and China these festivals are among the biggest of the year, creating mass movements of people as families gather from far and wide to observe them. While the festivals often involve calling on the ancestors for blessings, in some ways the event itself is also the blessing. The power and pull of the ancestors brings families together, in festivals that are as much about emotional bonding and support in the here-and-now as they are an occasion for remembering the departed.

Right: Bon Odori dances are performed at Obon festivals in Japan and lanterns guide spirits of ancestors.

Slavic Radonitsa

Find yourself in a Russian cemetery on the Tuesday after Easter (Pasha, in Russian), and you may be surprised to see people partying around the graves. Celebrated across the Slavic world, Radonitsa (Provody, in Ukraine) – 'Day of Rejoicing' – marks the end of Lent and the resurrection of Christ with a rousing commemoration of, and among, departed loved ones.

In ancient times, the Slavs of Eastern Europe celebrated the advent of spring with a graveside feast, joining their ancestors to give thanks for another winter survived. In Belarusian villages, people even brought tables to the cemeteries to place on top of family graves. As the Russian Orthodox Church grew in power and influence, the tradition evolved. Prayers were introduced, asking for the dead to join Christ in the afterlife and celebrating His resurrection by placing painted eggs on the graves of the departed. The eggs are sometimes served with honey and mead, the latter poured over the graves, according to Belarusian tradition.

Above: Radonitsa feast set up on a grave in Moldova.

Obon in Japan

In mid-August, trains from big cities like Tokyo and Osaka fill with people returning to their hometowns to celebrate Obon, a form of ancestor worship that sees families across Japan reunite to remember departed loved ones.

Cemeteries buzz as people deep-clean the family graves, leaving offerings of sweets, flowers and the deceased's favourite foods. Many people make so-called *shouryouma* ('spirit horses' made from whole cucumbers and aubergines with wooden-skewer legs) to place on graves, symbolically speeding along the ancestors' journeys to the family home.

On 13 August, people welcome ancestral spirits into their homes, often guiding the way with a small bonfire. Special offerings of food and flowers are placed at the ancestors' altars. The gathered family spends the next few days eating together and giving thanks to their ancestors – it's a time of deep bonding. Another bonfire marks the end of the festival on 16 August, sending the spirits back to their world.

Above: Obon prayers at Sanadayama Army Cemetery, Kyoto.

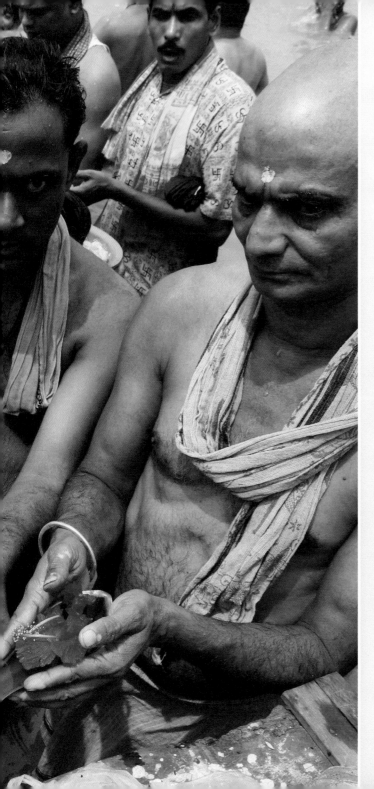

Pitru Paksha, India

Across much of India, in the Hindu lunar month of Bhadrapada (usually September), normal life comes to a halt for 16 days. Pitru Paksha is a time when families unite not only to pay homage to their ancestors, but to help them along their post-life journey. According to Hindu belief, the souls of three preceding generations dwell in Pitriloka, an in-between realm governed by Yama, the god of death. During Pitru Paksha, Yama frees the ancestors to accept offerings of food and water from their descendants – and this can help them escape and achieve *moksha* (enlightenment).

During Pitru Paksha, families perform a long list of rites, including reciting ancestors' names and preparing traditional foods like *kheer* (a sweet rice-and-milk pudding). The dishes are offered to a crow (representing Yama), a cow and a dog. When the crow has eaten, meaning that Yama has accepted the offering, the family can finally partake.

Hindu devotees perform Pitru Paksha rites on the banks of river Ganges, Kolkata.

Celtic Samhain

In Iron Age Scotland and Ireland, on the last night of October the doorways of the otherworld opened and the souls of the dead entered our world. Samhain marked the end of the harvest season and the start of winter, when the natural world started its annual dying off – a fitting time to honour the dead.

Hearthside places were set to welcome returning souls seeking hospitality. Bonfires blazed with sacrifices of crops and animals. Pranks were blamed on spirits that had sneaked in through the blurred border between worlds. People went from house to house disguised as the souls of the dead, singing or reciting verses in exchange for food.

With the spread of Catholicism, these pagan practices were repurposed. A celebration of Christian martyrs and saints called All Saints' Day – Allhallows in Middle English – was held on 1 November; the day before it, naturally, became All Hallows' Eve, and thus Samhain became what we know as Halloween.

Opposite: Modern-day pagans celebrate Samhain in Glastonbury. Right: A worshipper makes offerings at a park in Hong Kong during Hungry Ghost festival.

Hungry Ghost Festival, China

Every year on the 15th night of the lunar calendar's seventh month, the gates of the underworld open and ghosts are free to roam the living realm. This is a time to appease the wandering spirits – 'hungry ghosts' with insatiable appetites for food and attention – to stop them from disturbing the living. In reality, the Hungry Ghost Festival (known as Zhongyuan in Taoism and Yulanpen in Buddhism) is a month-long tradition of venerating the deceased – family ancestors, and all ancestors.

In Buddhist temples a feast is held with ritual food contributed by the community, while in family homes seats are added to the dinner table to welcome the departed. Incense and joss-paper offerings are burned in front of homes and at street corners. People pray and throw rice to feed unknown wandering ghosts, so that these homeless souls don't bring misfortune. Free theatre performances are staged, with the first row of seats kept empty to be claimed by spirit audience members.

COMMEMORATING

Subdued mourning CUSTOMS ARE OPTIONAL — we can choose INSTEAD TO SHOWCASE MEMORIES THAT BRING US DELIGHT.

ROMANIA'S MERRY CEMETERY

Grief comes in many colours. This kaleidoscopic cemetery in Romania teaches us to mourn with a skip in our step – and to remember the dead as they truly were.

The Merry Cemetery is a forest of blue crosses. Each is carved with lacy designs in the form of flowers, hearts and tiny crucifixes, ornamental lettering etched into the wood. In the middle of each cross is a painting in vivid colours, of someone working, cooking or maybe even smoking a cigarette.

For those accustomed to the Gothic tombs in most Eastern European cemeteries, this cheerful graveyard is a shock to the system. Across the Ukrainian border is Lychakiv Cemetery in Lviv, with weeping angels draped across mossy tombs. To the west in Budapest is Kerepesi Cemetery, where sombre mausoleums and tearful Madonnas remember the dead. Not so in the tiny village of Săpânța, northern Romania, where the unique cemetery has inspired the world, and attracted countless visitors.

CREATING A CEMETERY STYLE

The most common end-of-life customs in Romania are in the Orthodox tradition, involving a wake, a procession to the cemetery and pallbearers (usually from the dead person's family). Before the funeral, there is *priveghi* (a period of mourning), during which friends and family will watch over the body for three days, often drinking *țuică* (strong plum brandy) and eating *colivă* (a cake of boiled wheat and honey that is blessed and decorated with a cross).

During this time of togetherness, people share

REMEMBERING AUTHENTICALLY

'Don't speak ill of the dead.' This maxim aims to protect bereaved people from hearing hurtful words about the deceased, but it also censors us from honestly contemplating our memories. We often tell idealised stories when someone dies, extolling the deceased's virtues and forgetting their flaws. Romania's Merry Cemetery tells us that healthy grieving can welcome both.

The Merry Cemetery also shows us another way to feel when we visit burial sites. Cemeteries are generally places of lowered voices and reverent postures, but on a visit here you'll often see people chatting and laughing. Cultivating this atmosphere in other cemeteries would be a scandal, but here, Pătraş' unique memorials remind us that we can remember the dead with tears or with laughter. By visiting the Merry Cemetery and chuckling at someone's wry epitaph, we're sharing a joke with the dead. In our laughter, they live on.

stories about the deceased and improvise songs about their life.

In the 1930s, Săpânța sculptor Stan Ioan Pătraş (1908–1977) began to take inspiration from these mourning songs as he composed epitaphs for villagers'

graves. Before long, he was incorporating even salacious anecdotes into witty epitaphs.

LAUGHING THROUGH GRIEF

Pătraş began to develop a distinctive colour palette to

Above top: Epitaphs depict the lifestyles, even the vices, of the deceased.
Bottom: Wine is poured on funeral cake during an Orthodox ceremony.
Opposite: The workshop of sculptor Stan Ioan Pătraş at the Merry Cemetery.

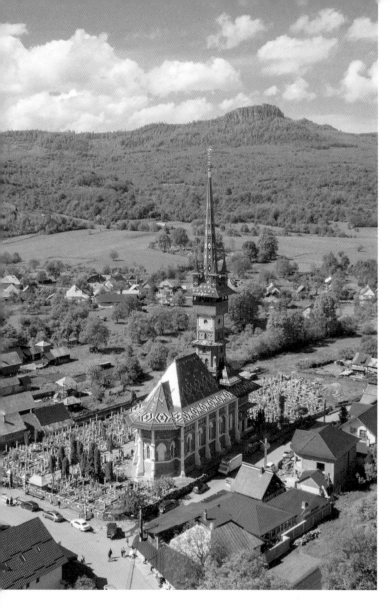

of blue, a colour he associated with hope, and added simple relief portraits of the deceased. He painted them with colours to represent the themes of their lives: red stood for love, yellow represented fertility, green symbolised life and vitality, while black indicated sorrow and death.

Walking around the cemetery today, you'll see epitaphs that offer teasing glimpses of villagers' lives, as well as some hilariously blunt descriptions. One warns passersby to be quiet, lest they wake the scolding mother-in-law buried here. Another jokes that the greatest joy of the deceased was to admire other men's wives in bars.

EPITAPHS BITTER & SWEET

Not all of Pătraș' etchings elicit mirth. Many are written from the perspective of the dead, some of them with a bitter, forlorn or even accusing tone; a few epitaphs curse the person responsible for their death.

The same duality is found in the naive-style art adorning each cross. One side might show the deceased doing what they loved: distilling brandy, cradling their child or managing their business. But the other might depict the way they died, even if they suffered a grisly death crushed by a train or beheaded in battle.

Pătraș also didn't shy away from depicting cruelty and

accompany these irreverent memorials. Each grave-marker in Săpânța's cemetery was an ornamental cross, carved out of oak from the forests of Maramureș. Pătraș started painting them a brilliant shade alcohol abuse, which allows some crosses to serve as cautionary tales. Whether sombre or titillating, above all Pătraş' crosses are honest.

Throughout his life, Pătraş hand-carved almost 800 crosses, including his own. When he died in 1977, his apprentice, Dumitru Pop Tincu, kept up the tradition. Pătraş' former studio is now a workshop filled with apprentices who continue his life's work. To locals, these sky-blue crosses are well worth the cost (roughly a month's salary).

UNFLINCHING ATTITUDES TO LIFE & DEATH
Some credit Romania's ancient history with this ability to appraise the lives of the dead dispassionately and honestly. Romania's earliest inhabitants, the Dacians, had a fearless attitude toward death due to the belief that they would meet Zalmoxis, their supreme deity, in the next life. Although Romania was Christianised from the 1st century CE, stoicism in the face of death lingers – especially in the country's most remote corners.

It's clear why this unadorned approach to remembering the dead endures in Săpânţa. This is a small village, where gossip spreads like wildfire. Locals are already well aware of their neighbours' habits and failings, so why varnish the truth when they die? By creating warts-and-all epitaphs and unflinching post-mortem portraits, Pătraş allowed the villagers to remember their dead as they truly were. And he gave his community a precious gift: the ability to laugh during times of sorrow.

SEE IT FOR YOURSELF

Săpânţa, in the northernmost tip of Maramureş, is right by the border with Ukraine, and hours from the towns on Romania's tourist trail, such as Bistriţa (2½ hours' drive away) and Cluj-Napoca (3½ hours' drive). You can visit by way of a long day-trip, or stop over in the pretty former gold-mining town of Baia Mare (1½ hours' drive from Săpânţa). It's very helpful to visit the cemetery with a Romanian-speaking guide at your side, to help translate and explain the epitaphs.

Be prepared for a tourist attraction as much as a burial ground, complete with five-lei entrance fee (double if you want to take photographs). This may feel uncomfortable, but know that locals have embraced the cemetery's appeal to travellers, and rely on tourist revenue to maintain the village and renovate the Church of the Nativity – an attractive Orthodox sanctuary with a teal-coloured roof. Be merry and feel free to take photographs, but remember this is a working cemetery: don't dress or pose in a way you would find tasteless if you saw it at your own family's grave.

Before you leave, visit Memorial House, the former home and studio of Stan Ioan Pătraş, now a museum in his honour. It's a short way down the road to the right of the main cemetery entrance.

MEMENTO MORI PHOTOGRAPHY

If death is but a sleep, photographs of the dead in peaceful repose can console us – and provide a visual focus for our grief.

Walking through a gallery, a black-and-white photograph catches your eye: a beautiful portrait of a child lying in her bed. There are pretty ribbons in her hair, the ruffles of her nightdress tickle her chin and her eyes are half-closed, as though she's about to drift off into sleep. You imagine the photo was taken while she slept, perhaps by adoring parents. But in fact, this is a post-mortem photograph: a portrait taken after someone's death.

These images are commonly known as memento mori photographs (from the Latin 'remember you will die'). Some capture a person in their coffin or in another ceremonial setting, perhaps surrounded by family members clutching wreaths. But they may also show the subject posed as though they are alive.

POSTHUMOUS PICTURES THROUGH HISTORY

Memento mori images long predate photography. From the Middle Ages, royal and noble families in Scandinavia, Western Europe and Russia commissioned paintings of deceased family members for 'mourning portraits'. Only the wealthiest could afford this expense, but the advent of photography allowed the upper-middle classes to take part.

In the 1890s, French inventor Louis-Jacques-Mandé Daguerre pioneered daguerreotype photography, in which a coated copper plate is exposed to vapours from iodine crystals

CAPTURING THE MOMENT

Grief is sharpened by a fear that our beloved will be forgotten, and photographs are a way to preserve memories of the dead. Nowadays, we generally have a trove of images to choose from. But before photography became routine, people turned to post-mortem portraits and photographs to maintain an emotional connection with the dead – something we now know is beneficial to the grieving process.

When someone we love dies, we feel their absence in our bodies: there's a hollowness in our stomach or chest, or difficulty in catching our breath. But expressing that feeling of absence is difficult, and physical objects can be an anchor. Whether photographs, letters or mementoes, these objects are the visual proof of someone's life, and they offer us a natural cue to talk about our dead loved ones. They can help us reconnect with a particular moment in time, making the departed seem less far away.

to produce an image from the resulting light-sensitive silver iodide. The process was relatively expensive, but it was nowhere near the price of commissioning paintings of the deceased, and post-mortem photography took off across Europe, North America and Australia.

IMAGES TO LAST CENTURIES

Most post-mortem photographs were for families. But for some famous figures, they could also communicate news of a death, or uphold a certain image of who the deceased was in life.

Argentine politician and activist Eva Perón was embalmed and photographed after her death, and images of her serenely beautiful face were widely circulated, giving a focal point for the country's grief. Victor Hugo appears wise and serene in his own post-mortem portrait, a profile shot where his forehead is bathed in light – most fitting for a luminary of French literature.

POSED FOR A FINAL SHOOT

A daguerreotype memento mori was considered an investment, and it might be the

Above: Photographs have long been a way of remembering the departed.
Opposite: Vanitas paintings like this one by Edwaert Collier were a
popular 17th-century form of memento mori – reminders of mortality.

only photograph ever taken of a person. The subject would be reclined on a sofa or laid in bed, or even propped up in a group family portrait. It's common to see images where the deceased is cradled by their parents or spouse, or has their hand held by a sibling. The photographer might even hand-paint eyes onto the final image, to give the appearance of life.

Daguerreotype photography required a long exposure, and the results weren't always crystal clear. One tell-tale sign that you're looking at a memento mori group photograph is that the living subjects may be slightly blurry whereas the motionless deceased will appear pin-sharp.

Today, post-mortem photographs still have an important role in memorialising the short lives of infants who are stillborn or die shortly after birth. But for the most part, the practice declined as it became easier and cheaper to take photographs of our daily lives. Whether photographs capture the living or the dead, they certainly have the power to make a moment in time – and our loved one – immortal.

REALMS OF BONE
Remarkable Catacombs & Ossuaries

From Roman-era mass tombs to the 'bone art' of ossuary artisans, these places have a meaning that transcends their function as mere skeleton depositories.

The first official catacomb was the system of underground tombs along Rome's Appian Way. Roman law forbade the burial of bodies within city limits — a sensible regulation that had been disposed with by medieval times, leading to untenable situations like that of 17th-century Paris, where city-centre burial grounds posed a real risk to the wellbeing of citizens.

Underground tunnels and crypts — either purpose-built or reclaimed — became an expedient and elegant solution to the problem of excess skeletons. (A lexicographical note: a catacomb is underground, while an ossuary is simply a place where bones are kept.) While at heart an operational affair, these realms of bone often take on deeper significance.

As grand-scale memento mori, they remind us of life's fleeing nature, that in death we are all alike. As an engraving in the Paris Catacombs says: 'So all things pass upon the Earth / Spirit, beauty, grace, talent / Ephemeral as a flower / Tossed by the slightest breeze.'

Opposite: decorative skulls and bones at Sedlec Ossuary, Czech Republic.

Sedlec Ossuary

An unprepossessing chapel beneath the Cemetery Church of All Saints in Kutná Hora, about 56km (35 miles) east of Prague, is perhaps the world's most celebrated 'bone church'.

The story begins with a pilgrimage to the Holy Land. When a local abbot returned with holy soil that he sprinkled on the cemetery here, he made it the most sought-after burial ground in all of 13th-century Bohemia. When the plague came in the 14th century, the influx of bodies became unmanageable, and the ossuary was constructed in around 1400 to make room in the fast-filling cemetery.

In 1870 a notable family in the area appointed local artist and carpenter František Rint to reorganise the chaotic, full-to-bursting chapel. He created a macabre wonderland, making works of art from cleaned and polished human bones: the notable family's coat of arms, an ornate chalice, and the proud artist's signature spelled out in bone. Garlands of skulls festoon the arches surrounding the crowning masterpiece: a vast, ornate chandelier that uses every bone in the human body.

Right: around 40,000 human skeletons adorn Sedlec Ossuary.

Paris Catacombs

The story of Paris' Catacombs is a tale of urban overcrowding. By the late 1700s, the city's medieval cemeteries were bursting at the seams, making life increasingly unpleasant for nearby residents: undrinkable well-water, noxious smells and the occasional resurfacing of buried corpses.

A solution presented itself in the 241km (150 miles) of disused limestone quarries that underlay the city streets. Beginning in 1785, the bones of between six- and seven-million people – the oldest dating back over 1200 years – were moved five storeys underground. It took 12 years.

By 1860, when it finally closed to burials, the Paris Municipal Ossuary had already become a popular tourist attraction. It had opened to the public in 1809, with a touch of macabre drama contributed by engraved signs such as '*Arrête! C'est ici l'empire de la mort*' ('Stop! This is the empire of death').

Part public health measure, part urban engineering feat, part sign of respect for the long-since departed, the Catacombs are now the world's most visited memento mori, with over half a million annual visitors being reminded of the ephemeral nature of life.

Above: Paris' Catacombs hold the bones of the city's medieval residents.

Catacombs of Kom Ash Shuqqaf

Once Egypt's capital city, Alexandria was dubbed the 'Paris of Antiquity', a multicultural melting pot and a vital crossing point between Asia and Europe. When an unfortunate donkey fell down a shaft here in 1900, it led to the discovery of an underground necropolis reflecting the interment traditions of three great cultures.

Used as a burial chamber from the 2nd to 4th centuries CE, the Catacombs of Kom Ash Shuqqaf are considered one of the Seven Wonders of the Medieval World. With sarcophagi for the placement of Egyptian mummies alongside niches for the remains of those who opted for Greek- and Roman-style cremation, the catacombs attest to the contemporary commingling of funerary traditions. And of art: on one tomb, statues of a man and woman are carved in stiff Egyptian poses, while the man's head is chiselled in the lifelike Greek style and the woman sports an unmistakably Roman hairstyle. Also Roman is the triclinium, or banquet room, where relatives held annual ceremonial feasts to honour their dead.

Above: Kom Ash Shuqqaf unites art and traditions from the Eyptian, Greek and Roman civilisations.

Catacombs of Lima

A monumental complex in Lima's historical centre, the Convento San Francisco is a jewel of Peru's viceroyalty era. Inaugurated in 1672, the convent's cavernous underground vaults were the colonial city's first and largest cemetery, with up to 75,000 bodies estimated to have been buried here. When overcrowding became an issue, corpses were dissolved in quicklime, leaving only the skeletons.

Forgotten for over a century, the catacombs were rediscovered in 1943. They are said to be connected by subterranean passageways to the cathedral, other local churches and even the Government Palace. Some believe they may have been used during the Inquisition.

Caretakers here took an artistic approach to the storage of their skeletal guests. Many of the bones are stacked in patterns — seen from the viewing grates above, they resemble mandalas, with skulls and femurs forming concentric rings. Other bones are classified by type and neatly stacked together, tibia with tibia, cranium with cranium.

Right: Bones in the Lima Catacombs are artfully arranged.

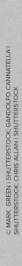

Palermo's Capuchin Monastery Catacombs

When brother Silvestro da Gubbio died in 1599, there was no room to bury him in the crowded cemetery of the Capuchin order's Palermo monastery. So the monks began to excavate the crypts below. Initially only for deceased friars, burial in the Catacombe dei Cappuccini became a sign of prestige, the costly upkeep of the bodies payable only by the wealthiest citizens.

Over the years, the monks perfected the art of preservation: bodies were dried in special rooms, bathed in a vinegar solution and stuffed with hay. Mummification was a way to keep the dead close, says Dario Piombino-Mascali, archaeologist with the Sicily Mummy Project. "In Sicily, death has always been part of life. For centuries many Sicilians used mummification to make sure there was a constant relationship between life and death."

This ossuary with a difference is the final resting place for 8000 corpses and 1252 mummies, dressed up to the nines and displayed like life-sized dolls: hung from walls, perched on benches, set in poses. The halls are divided by category: men, women, virgins, children, priests, monks, professionals. Brother Silvestro da Gubbio is still there, greeting visitors at the entrance.

Above: The Capuchin Catacombs are today a macabre tourist attraction.

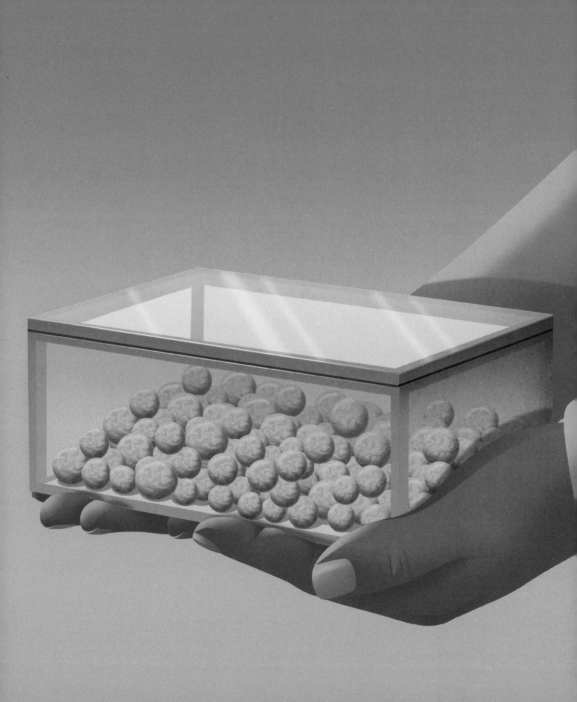

KOREA'S CREMATION BEADS

Created from crystallised ashes, shimmering strings of 'death beads' are a lustrous memorial keepsake for increasing numbers of Korean people – and for the bereaved all over the world.

More and more Koreans are choosing sparkling mementoes over sombre urns and graves. Known as cremation beads or death beads, these tiny orbs are made from human ashes that have been ground down and superheated until they crystallise. They're then shaped and polished into shiny beads, which can emerge bluish black, emerald green or even violet. The final result is a trove of glittering gems, which the family can store at home or thread onto a string to wear as jewellery.

CHANGING DEATH CUSTOMS

Death beads began as a creative response to the practical necessity of limited burial space. Twenty years ago, burial in a cemetery was the most common practice, but given the country's huge population (over 51.7 million people), South Korea's government decided to introduce a law requiring families to exhume remains from graveyards after a period of 60 years. This fuelled a dramatic reversal in end-of-life choices: nowadays less than 30% of Koreans opt for burials.

As cremations increased, Koreans faced a dilemma: what to do with the ashes? Scattering ashes is common around the world, but this practice has a mixed reception among Korean people. Confucianism urges the living to honour the dead, and the idea of casting aside someone's remains makes some Koreans uncomfortable. Noticing

GRIEF NEEDS AN ANCHOR

Physical objects can act as an anchor during grief's most turbulent moments. When a memory of a departed loved one appears in our minds, grief can crash against us with the force of a tidal wave – making us feel disoriented, hopeless and desperately missing our loved one's touch. At times like this, touching death beads (or any object associated with the deceased) can provide a comforting focus, and create a moment of closeness and relief.

No wonder that the practice of transforming ashes has spread far beyond South Korea. People's ashes can be turned into pebbles, polished smooth to be cupped in your hand. They can be captured inside decorative glass orbs, or turned into diamonds that you can wear as jewellery – eternally keeping someone close to your skin. Carrying someone in your heart can be lonely and heavy; but in a strange way, literally carrying them can lighten the burden.

this unease, and people's desire for alternatives to the static, unyielding form of urns, enterprising companies began to produce beads made of ashes.

INNOVATION BORN FROM NECESSITY

Several South Korean companies offer the service, though production methods vary. Some add minerals to improve the beads' appearance, while other companies, such as Bonhyang – a name referencing a god that oversees family trees – pride themselves on creating death beads made exclusively from human ashes.

In South Korea today, strings of these twinkling baubles are run through fingers or treasured in glass cases: a beautiful and tactile focal point for remembrance.

Above: Funeral candles in South Korea. Opposite: Tombstones in Seoul National Cemetery. Burial space in South Korea is at a premium.

SOUTH KOREA'S ELEMENTAL DEATH RITES

Shamanism and Confucianism intermingle to influence South Korean death customs, highly intentional about end-of-life care and strongly informed by *pungsu-jiri* (literally, 'wind-water-earth principles').

A 'good death' happens under the eye of the family, and preparations begin even before someone's life ends. A dying person is taken to their home. Not only are they comforted by familiar surroundings, but this ensures their spirit will not wander, lost, after death – which is considered unlucky for the entire community.

Immediately after death, the family may collectively wail or cry; in the past, this was a way to announce a death to the wider community. The body is washed in fragrant water, the ears and nose plugged with cotton, and coins placed over the eyes. Rice is placed inside the mouth, to represent a plentiful afterlife, and the body is shrouded in white.

As offerings to messengers from the other world, three bowls of rice, of soup and of vegetables are prepared, and three pairs of shoes are set outside the home.

For those who aren't cremated, their burial location is determined according to *pungsu-jiri*. The ideal location is flanked by hills and mountains, with natural water nearby – a peaceful and scenic place for their final repose.

SAMSUNG

MTN

Menu   ◉   Name

OK/2̃

C

1∞   2abc   3def

4ghi   5jkl   6mno

7pqrs   8tuv   9wxyz

*↑   0+   #

SAMSUNG

GHANA'S FANTASY COFFINS

Want to ride into the eternal sunset aboard an eagle, or in a bright yellow sports car? The makers of Ghana's fantasy coffins think outside the box, building caskets in every imaginable shape.

A funeral procession pours along the streets of Accra. Almost everyone is clad in Ghana's traditional red and black mourning colours, and they're carrying the coffin closer and closer. That's when you notice there is a curious winged vessel being carried aloft by the crowd... Is it a bird, is it a plane? Neither: it's a 'fantasy coffin', also known as a FAV (Fantastic Afterlife Vehicle).

When it comes to unorthodox transportation to the afterlife, nothing comes close to Ghana's fantasy coffins. For more than 70 years, Ghanaian artists have been chiselling coffins shaped like ships, chilli peppers or airplanes. Any object even vaguely oblong in shape can inspire a unique creation – made to order by one of a dozen FAV makers in Ghana (mostly around the capital, Accra).

TOTEMIC PROTECTION

The originator of fantasy coffins is Kane Kwei, who established a coffin workshop in the 1950s and passed on his unmistakable style and craft to many apprentices. But the concept dates back much further, to *okadi akpakai*: palanquins (wheelless litters) that were used to carry kings and sub-chiefs of the Ga people.

Palanquins took the shape of the owner's totem, a symbolic object or animal; being transported inside *okadi akpakai* was believed to guarantee protection. Local stories tell of a chief who died before he could be paraded around in his cocoa-

PORTRAIT OF A LIFE

Imagine throwing a party for a friend who's moving overseas. You're sad that they're leaving, and you wish you'd had more time; but you're eager to celebrate everything they've meant to you. You put Champagne on ice, invite friends and family and have one glorious final knees-up before they get on that plane.

This is the sentiment behind Ghanaian funerals: sorrow cuts deep, but the funeral doesn't need to be a sombre affair. People will weep and mourn, but they'll also joke, dance and feast. After all, we live our lives in technicolour, so why not our deaths?

When we lose someone, it can be upsetting if our final image of that person is a blank coffin lowered into the ground. In Ghana, instead it can be a bright totem representing something they held dear. Subdued mourning customs are optional; we can choose to showcase treasured memories that bring us delight.

pod-shaped palanquin, so he was buried inside it instead. This is believed to have inspired Kwei's fantasy coffins, which quickly became an Accra funeral fixture.

A ROYAL SENDOFF

Fantastical coffins are no longer reserved for royals, and nor do they need to be modelled on traditional totems. Today, their shape is only limited by your imagination. You can be buried inside a giant palm fruit, or meet eternity in a pen-shaped casket. You can send your dad to heaven in a beer-bottle-shaped casket, or bury your stern auntie inside a hawk in flight.

If the deceased was pious (or you just want to ensure the pastor allows the coffin into church for the funeral ceremony), you can opt for a Bible-shaped coffin. But

Above: Fantasy coffins are hand-carved and hand-painted.
Opposite top: Coffin maker Eric Kpakpo sits in front of a $100 bill-shaped coffin at his workshop in Accra.
Bottom: A coffin shaped as a fishing boat, crafted for a fisher.

it's most common for a fantasy coffin to represent something the deceased enjoyed in life, like a wine bottle, a sneaker, a mobile phone or a cigarette. The coffin might even represent the dead person's dreams and ambitions, and act as the final fulfilment of their aspirations in life.

EXQUISITE TASTE

Accra's coffin workshops are a riot of hammering, sawing and swishing paintbrushes, as artists busily assemble and decorate oversized insects, fish and ears of corn. With this standard of craft, it takes at least a couple weeks to create a bespoke

Above: Coffins can come in any form imaginable. Opposite: A mermaid coffin for a tribal priestess is carried by funeral guests in Teshie.

THE ART OF MOURNING

The main drawback of being buried in a fantasy coffin? You won't get to admire it for yourself. But even if you never make it to Ghana, you can still see elaborate FAVs in galleries around the world. The largest permanent exhibition of fantasy coffins can be found at the National Museum of Funeral History in Houston, Texas.

Several artists have become celebrities in the coffin creation world. Some, like Ataa Oko, kept their styles typically Ghanaian. But others have flung open their arms to collaborations with European artists, such as Kudjoe Affutu, whose work has been displayed in Hamburg, Paris and Monaco.

The most famous living artist is Paa Joe; his creations can cost up to US$15,000 and are shipped overseas to delight a vast international clientele. A former apprentice of coffin-art visionary Kane Kwei, Paa Joe has amassed almost 16,000 Instagram followers and has been visited by former US president Bill Clinton; his fantastical coffins have been displayed at exhibitions as far afield as Paris and New York.

Paa Joe's apprentice, Daniel 'Hello' Mensah, has also risen to prominence. Coffins created in his studio in Teshie, southeastern Ghana, have been showcased in London's British Museum.

just one component of a lavish celebration of life, where the festivities' extravagance is a tribute to the dead. Attendees often bring donations to give to the grieving family. Crowds will gather, including people who may have had no relationship with the deceased, to follow a funeral procession that might include paid mourners (page 160). Some funerals even have dancing pallbearers, who transport the coffin with a variety of eclectic dancing styles: rhythmically crawling with the coffin on their backs, or performing choreographed moves while holding the coffin aloft. The procession and burial are often followed by up to three days of celebration, complete with feasting, live music or a DJ.

Many Ghanaians believe that fantasy coffins will remind the dead person of their passions and talents when they arrive in the spiritual realm. It's also believed that your ancestors have the power to influence your fate on Earth, so it's important to keep them happy after death – making springing for that expensive Porsche coffin a prudent decision.

coffin – and demand for these premium products is at sky-high levels.

Most locals spend the equivalent of US$1000, but coffin makers increasingly take commissions from people overseas who are willing to pay a premium, including art collectors around the world. One Porsche-shaped fantasy coffin sold for an impressive US$9200 at London auction house Bonhams, and even former US president Jimmy Carter is believed to have purchased a Ghanaian FAV.

BRIGHTENING THE AFTERLIFE

In Ghana, a body typically spends weeks in refrigerated storage while the family makes extensive funeral preparations. This gives artists plenty of time to fashion the coffin: perhaps a snarling lion, or a shiny black dress shoe. Death is viewed as preparation for a journey, so it's logical to equip a loved one with a vessel that is suitably grand, and reflective of their personality and status.

When the day of the funeral arrives, typically a Saturday, the unveiling of the fantasy coffin is

Above: Traditional performers honour a former Ghanaian footballer in Accra.

THE FANTASY COFFIN ARTIST

Eric Adjetey Anang runs the Kane Kwei Carpentry Workshop in Accra, Ghana.

coffin is a serious thing for the family, and as soon as they commission you, you must be serious. It's a back-and-forth. You are playing with the design, exaggerating and adjusting it as you go, and that's what I love about it.

The customer is not just a customer, they become part of the family. They have to trust you. They've lost a dear one and by the time they come to you, they are grieving, they are mourning. If the person was young I might feel sad, but if they are older that's fine — it's a celebration of life and that's why I'm there. My job is to build a house for the body of someone who has made a good living. It's celebrating a life well-lived.

I built my own coffin 10 years ago. My dad didn't like the idea — he said you're too young, it's not your turn to die! I always tell him, if there one thing you should fight over it's your coffin, that's the construction that you take with you when you go. My coffin will be a wooden hand-plane — I always have one with me wherever I travel.

Kane Kwei is my grandfather. He built the workshop and lived there until 1992 when he passed away. I grew up in the house where the workshop was, so I would see them doing everything by hand — cutting the wood, planing it — everything done with hand-tools. In 2005 I took over the of management of the shop.

What do I love about my profession? The smell of the wood! I see what I do as construction — it's like a puzzle, putting all the little pieces of wood together. In the beginning you have a model, at the same time you are planning how you want it to go as you build. The

REUNITING WITH THE DEAD IN SULAWESI

Not only do the Torajan people keep their dead close and put on grand funerals, they periodically exhume the bodies to show reverence and love for generations past.

Imagine caring for a frail relative. By night, you make sure their head is resting comfortably on their pillow. And by day, you're attentive to their every need: dressing them, combing their hair, preparing their favourite foods. When the rest of the family isn't looking, you might even buy their preferred brand of cigarettes and place one between their lips.

This is exactly how the Torajan people of South Sulawesi care for their dead. In the highlands of this island province in Indonesia, people extend the same gentle caretaking to the dead that they would perform during life.

FLAMBOYANT FUNERALS

A funeral ceremony might not take place for years after a person's physical death, allowing the family to save for a suitably grand finale. Until then, the newly dead are considered to occupy a twilight state between this life and Puya, the land of the spirits. They remain members of the household and are referred to as 'sleeping' or 'unwell'. The family will speak to the body of their relative, symbolically feed them and take them outside the home.

When the funeral finally arrives, the family will sacrifice chickens and water buffalo, which are believed to carry the deceased into the next life. It's a grand and costly event, and an opportunity for descendants to symbolically 'pay forward' the investment the deceased made by raising and caring for them in life.

DEATH IS NOT AN ENDING

When we treat death like an abrupt change of state, while still experiencing grief as an ongoing process, the disconnect can be disorienting and painful. But the Torajan people don't consider death to be a singular event: it's a gradual transformation that begins with the death of the physical body. The relationship between the living and the deceased doesn't end, it simply transforms from actively socialising with them to relating to them as an ancestor. The period of caring for a body before a funeral allows grieving relatives to move slowly between those two states.

Even long after the funeral, the festival of Ma'Nene offers people the chance of a reunion, whether their loved ones died recently or decades ago. This ritual is more than a balm for grief: it helps the whole community face death with less fear. They know they will be cared for and remembered long after they're gone.

MA'NENE: RECONNECTING WITH THE DEAD

The Torajan people's death customs are so well known in South Sulawesi that they attract curious outsiders. Some rituals are even publicised on tourism websites – particularly the Ma'Nene festival, which takes place every one to three years in August or September.

People from South Sulawesi travel from all around Indonesia to return to their home villages for Ma'Nene. First, the family forms a procession to the burial house

Above: A Torajan funeral ceremony. Opposite top: Relatives and friends gather in a circle. Middle: Elaborate traditional coffins contribute to funeral costliness. Bottom: In Tana Toraja coffins are placed in caves with balconies adorned by wooden statues.

where they will collect the bodies of their ancestors. Bodies are laid out in the sun to dry, while the crypt is given a thorough spring-cleaning. Next, the dead are treated to the kindness and care that you would extend to an ailing relative: they are cleaned with water and given fresh clothing, often made from the finest materials (or perhaps the office clothing they wore in life, or their old military uniform).

These customs stem from an old legend about a hunter, Pong Rumasek, who found a dead body in the mountains. Pong Rumasek cared for the body and clothed it in his own garments, and was rewarded with luck. This association between care of the dead and good fortune in life has endured: the Torajan people believe that if the spirits of the dead are unhappy, they'll make this known with a bad harvest.

Relatives often take photographs with the spruced-up bodies, holding them up for a family portrait, and walking with them around the village. Seeing their stiff but colourfully and carefully dressed forms from a distance, propped up against walls or tightly clasped by their living relatives, you could almost mistake them for being alive.

PAPUA NEW GUINEA'S PROTECTOR MUMMIES

Among certain highland tribes in Papua New Guinea, the dead remain ever-present. Their bodies are smoked, and these modern-day mummies keep a watchful eye over their descendants.

From a distance, it's difficult to tell if the guard's wide-open jaw signals horror or surprise. What makes it even harder is the skin peeling away from his skull. He's one of several mummified corpses watching over his village in Papua New Guinea – preserved post-mortem in a painstaking process of smoking the body.

Using smoke to mummify the dead is now vanishingly rare in PNG, but the practice continues in remote parts of the Highlands, particularly among the Angu people. Souls of the dead are believed to roam outside the body by day and return to the body at night, to keep watch over their descendants. When bodies aren't correctly mummified their spirits may become restless and cause crops to fail; but when treated with care, they can be asked for advice and guard over the community from high cliffs.

MUMMIFICATION, PAST & PRESENT

Mummification is synonymous with ancient Egyptians, who carefully embalmed, shrouded and safeguarded their dead in underground tombs. But numerous ancient cultures have also made use of the practice – like the Inca (who mummified high-ranking members of society), and people in ancient China (the Tarim Basin mummies date back to 1800 BCE).

THE SENTINEL DEAD

For people foreign to Papua New Guinea, it may be stomach-churning to learn how some tribes smoke, pierce and showcase their dead. But how much of this revulsion depends on whether body preservation takes place in plain sight?

In the US, more than half of the country's dead are embalmed: cleaned, drained of fluids and injected with formaldehyde. Incisions are made in the abdomen, and facial features are set using wires and glues. Mummification in PNG happens while the family looks on; in the US it takes place behind closed doors at a funeral home, the deceased's family only seeing the end result: their preserved, smartly dressed loved one inside a coffin.

The benefits of these customs aren't dissimilar. We may experience closure when faced with the body of a departed loved one, and find consolation in the idea that they watch over us after death. In remote parts of PNG, the watching is simply more literal.

What's less well-known is that mummification isn't in the past. PNG is far from the only place in Southeast Asia to mummify its dead — families also smoke their dead in some mountainous parts of the Philippines (page 215), while the Torajan people of Indonesia (page 95) dry out the bodies of their loved ones. There are mummified bodies in European cultures, too, like Capuchin crypts in Palermo, Sicily (page 81) and Brno in the Czech Republic.

SMOKING THE CORPSE
Soon after death, the deceased person's body is placed in a

Above: Above: The Anga tribe of Papua New Guinea's remote Highlands mummify their deceased loved ones according to tribal law, by suspending them over a smoking fire for many weeks.

mummification chair and its limbs are tied to the frame. The chair is suspended over a fire and smoked for one to three months. When the body swells, it is punctured with a wooden stick to let fluids drain out. These bodily fluids may be rubbed onto the bodies of mourners, and some will even refrain from washing themselves throughout the entire grieving process.

Once mummification is complete, the now-leathery and smoke-stained body is taken up to an elevated place like a cliff, where it joins other mummies in watching over the community.

UNDER THE WATCHFUL EYE OF ANCESTORS

Across PNG's diverse regions and tribes, mummification is just one custom that accompanies death. It's common for a community to spend several days commemorating a death and singing mourning songs. Women who lose their husbands daub their faces in grey clay and, in rare cases, practise finger amputation (p145). But mummification is one of the most visible parts of PNG's death customs because of the final destination of the bodies: overlooking the village from a high perch.

The Aseki district has numerous sites where you can see mummies only a short distance from villages and roads. Some locals charge tourists a small fee to be guided to see these grinning skeletons peering out from above.

CIMETIÈRE DES CHIENS

1899

ALTER
EGO

PET CEMETERIES

All around the world, furry friends are laid to rest beneath tiny headstones. But pet cemeteries aren't a modern phenomenon: the world's most ancient cultures spared no expense when memorialising animals.

Walking through a cemetery, you notice an ornate tombstone beneath a willow tree. Curious, you stoop to examine the inscription, and the simple epitaph reads: 'Here Lies Spot'.

Burying animals with the same solemnity as humans can seem peculiar, or even taboo. But pet cemeteries have been rising in popularity since the 19th century, and animals have been interred with ceremony for many thousands of years.

Ancient animal burials have been excavated as far and wide as the Middle East, Siberia and North America, and some Stone Age archaeological sites have revealed humans and dogs buried together as far back as 14,000 years ago.

In Ancient Egypt, many domestic animals were honoured with the same burial traditions as their owners, including mummification. Scholars believe that mummified cats were given as ritual offerings to the cat-

headed goddess of protection, Bastet; but many ancient Egyptians also believed that their beloved pets could join them in the next life.

MOURNING A FURRY FAMILY MEMBER

Over in Europe, it took until 1881 for official pet cemeteries to appear. This was the year a Maltese terrier named Cherry was buried in the back garden of Victoria Lodge in London's Hyde Park. The gatekeeper had

HONOUR EVERY KIND OF LOSS

Creatures great and small are woven into the fabric of our societies, and pet cemeteries remind us of how they enrich our lives. The death of an adored pet can be as devastating as losing a family member. Your life can be upended by the loss of daily routines like feeding and walking, not to mention being deprived of their companionship. Anyone who places this grief on a lower tier simply hasn't experienced the unconditional love of a labrador, or the delight of coming home to a precocious kitten.

Then there are the heroic contributions made by animals. Exploring pet cemeteries, you'll see tombs for service animals, rescue dogs and police dogs; London's Ilford Animal Cemetery is the final resting place of military animals, including carrier pigeons. Animals that play crucial roles – carrying messages, saving lives, even sniffing out cancer – warrant funerals with pomp and lasting memorials.

taken pity on Cherry's grieving owners, who wanted their dog laid to rest in his favourite place. Cherry was swiftly joined by many others; pets were starting to be considered fully fledged members of a household, rather than simply performing duties like guarding or hunting.

But humankind's love for animals can reach much greater heights than mere tombs. Alexander the Great named an entire city, Peritas, in memory of his mastiff, and planted a statue of his pet in the main square – and we'd wager that most dog-lovers would do the same.

Above: Good boys, even in death. Opposite: Edinburgh's famous Greyfriars Bobby.

SEE IT FOR YOURSELF

You could travel right across Europe on a pet-cemetery-themed itinerary. Start in Edinburgh's Greyfriars Kirkyard to see the UK's most famous pet grave. It's the resting place of a Skye terrier, Bobby, who became a parable of loyalty after watching over his master's grave for 14 years, until his own death in 1872. Next, board a train to London and tour historic Hyde Park Secret Pet Cemetery,

before hopping on the Eurostar. Northwest of Paris in Asnières-sur-Seine, stroll through the Cimetière des Chiens et Autres Animaux Domestiques (Cemetery of Dogs and Other Household Animals). Since 1899, mourners have buried horses, cats and even goldfish here.

The US also has several intriguing destinations, including the world's oldest operating pet cemetery. More than 70,000 furry and feathered friends have been buried in Hartsdale Pet Cemetery,

New York, since it opened in 1896. See the gravestone of a lion cub (the pet of a Hungarian princess) and a Jack Russell terrier named Clarence (the pet of a singer-songwriter, Mariah Carey). Over in LA, the Hollywood Forever Cemetery has lavish tombs in memory of celebrity dogs such as Strongheart, one of Hollywood's first-ever canine actors; and Terry, the terrier who played Toto in *The Wizard of Oz* (1939).

ALTERNATIVE FAREWELLS

Go out with a bang...or a splash, roar or rumble. Alternative funerals offer spectacular sendoffs to people with deep pockets, and these end-of-life ceremonies draw inspiration from ancient history and sci-fi.

Death doesn't need to be your final journey. With an alternative funeral, your remains can take an odyssey into deep water or even deep space. You can live on as a gemstone, string of beads (p83) or a coral reef. Or you can attempt to avoid the Reaper altogether, making a last bid for immortality in a cryogenic chamber.

A MIGHTY SENDOFF

There's an extraordinary range of alternatives to traditional burials and cremations. Some people take their cues from the past, like outlandish actor Nicolas Cage, who has looked to Ancient Egypt and commissioned his own burial pyramid. Meanwhile, some funeral parlours offer small-scale Viking-style sea burials. Setting a body on fire and launching it out onto water on a longship would be illegal in most places, though it's possible to have a symbolic alternative by setting alight a packet of ashes, or a lock of hair, on a miniature vessel.

But most alternative funerals have an eye on the future, finding innovative ways to dispose of – or conserve – human bodies.

SLEEP WITH THE FISHES

It's common to scatter ashes at sea, forever commingling a loved one with nature. But with a little help from Eternal Reefs, human ashes can be mixed into concrete and formed into a 'reef ball' to actively sustain sea life. Within a few weeks, microorganisms will burrow and grow on these hollow,

GOING OUT IN STYLE

Making a bold statement through your choice of funeral is the ultimate in having the last word. After all, why slip offstage quietly when you can take a flamboyant bow?

Nonetheless, most of us likely consider being shot out of a cannon or buried inside a giant marble pyramid to be darkly amusing thought experiments, rather than end-of-life rituals we'll actually pursue. In reality, we're often constrained by finances, local norms, religious traditions or family conventions. But it's still seductive to imagine that when we die we can deliver one final moment of awe and surprise.

This urge to assert our individuality, or even defy expectations, reveals as much about our lives as our deaths. Would an unconventional sendoff be a fitting reflection of your life? Or does the allure of an extraordinary funeral signal that you're burning to achieve and experience so much more while you're still alive?

vented spheres, and they'll soon be aflutter with angelfish and fan-shaped feather duster worms.

While it's the structure of the ball, rather than the human ashes, that supports marine life, spending eternity as a coral reef has a poetic appeal – plus you're spending money on ocean conservation rather than a casket or headstone.

THE FINAL FUNERARY FRONTIER

While the ocean has a tranquil appeal, others dream of boldly going into space. The first ever such burial was in 1992, when

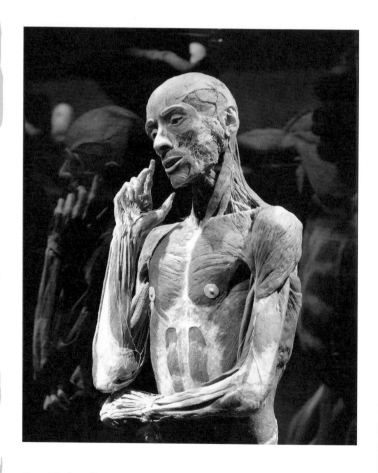

Above: Plastinated human at a Body Worlds exhibition. Opposite: As Eternal Reefs' reef balls mature, they become permanent additions to the underwater environment, developing and supporting marine life.

Star Trek creator and screenwriter Gene Roddenberry's cremains were launched into space. Only five years later, 24 people's ashes were carried aboard a *Pegasus* rocket and sent into orbit before hurtling back down to Earth. The company behind these inaugural space burials, Celestis, now offers an end-to-end multiday memorial, including a service and viewing the launch of a loved one's remains — either on a short space flight, right to the moon, or even into deep space.

Beyond Burials also offer different tiers of service: your ashes can be shot into space on a suborbital rocket, spending a few minutes in microgravity before hurtling back to Earth; or they can be scattered in space from a low-Earth orbit rocket, after which they circle the Earth before re-entering the atmosphere. Or you can mingle with moondust and spend eternity watching our blue planet from afar: some rockets will take your cremains to the moon and deposit ashes on its rocky surface.

And if you want an explosive experience without the otherworldly price tag, you can have your ashes mixed with fireworks. Gonzo journalist Hunter S Thompson famously had his own ashes blasted from a cannon, with Hollywood stars including Jack Nicholson and Bill Murray watching the fiery display.

Above top: A Viking longship burns at Shetland's Up Helly Aa festival.
Bottom: Nicolas Cage's burial pyramid in New Orleans.

PLASTIC FANTASTIC

If you don't want to burn out or fade away, you can choose a modern alternative to mummification. Developed by Gunther von Hagens in the 1970s, plastination involves replacing a body's natural liquids and fats with plastics, preserving them from within as durable anatomical specimens – and although more than 20,000 people have signed up, he's always looking for new body donors.

Think of plastination as an extreme form of embalming. First, formaldehyde is pumped through your body to halt decomposition. Next, your skin and connective tissues are carefully removed to conserve your body's structure. Your body's water and fats are dissolved with acetone and you're bathed in liquid polymer, which penetrates the cells. Finally, you're put in position and cured with light, heat or gas.

Von Hagens displays his specimens for educational purposes, but his style borders on macabre modern art. Your plastinated body might be placed on top of a bike, or given an athletic pose, with your skin splayed open to reveal every muscle and sinew.

Ever since the first ever exhibition of plastinated bodies in Japan, collections of these preserved cadavers have featured in Body Worlds exhibitions from London to Los Angeles. Some might do it for posthumous fame (the exhibitions have been viewed by more than 50 million people so far). But others are drawn to von Hagens' mission: to help people understand the beauty and fragility of the human body, before it's too late.

CHEATING DEATH WITH CRYONICS

Go to sleep in a freezer, get thawed out centuries later, and then proceed to be cured of all ailments by the latest technological advances. Cryopreservation of human bodies has a clear narrative in sci-fi, but scientists haven't developed techniques to successfully reanimate a frozen body...yet.

Silicon Valley billionaires, such as PayPal cofounder Peter Thiel are signing up for cryopreservation and betting that technology might win out over human mortality. After all, medical innovations like ventilators and defibrillators can bring a human back from the brink of death; who's to say that in centuries to come we won't be capable of much more?

Cryopreservation is illegal in some countries, and unregulated in others. In the US, you can 'donate' your body for the purpose, though some cryonics contracts have been successfully challenged in court. But if you gamble tens of thousands of dollars on the hope of immortality, your body will be cooled, massaged and kept oxygenated shortly after death. Next, an antifreeze solution will be pumped into your bloodstream to avoid ice crystallisation damaging your body. You're then cooled in a nitrogen vapour chamber, and finally stored in a vessel resembling an oversized shiny thermos. See you in the year 3000...

PRESERVING HEROES FOR ETERNITY

Many of us aspire to immortality, but some Communist leaders have achieved it – at least in physical form. National heroes from Lenin to Mao Zedong lie on public display, as monuments to big ideas.

When you visit Moscow's Red Square, the Kremlin humbles and St Basil's Cathedral dazzles – but the sight everyone talks about is Lenin's Mausoleum. After the founding father of the Soviet Union passed away in 1924, his body was permanently exhibited in a granite tomb, tucked up against the walls of the Kremlin. He lies there still, waxy and immutable, and preserved for almost a century by teams of expert embalmers.

Some 2.5 million visitors file through the doors of Lenin's tomb every year, and the paying of respect is strictly enforced. Attendants are constantly on hand to make sure visitors doff hats, remove hands from pockets and maintain a dignified silence as they file silently past the milky-white cadaver. You don't need to be a card-carrying Communist to appreciate the continued reverential devotion to this long-dead revolutionary.

ACHIEVING IMMORTALITY

For those from outside Russia, visiting Lenin's tomb is like stepping into a David Lynch dream, an effect exaggerated by the deep shadows and two-tone colour scheme – black and Communist red, of course – inside the darkened chamber. For locals, the experience is more profound: it's a way to connect with a time when Russia was on the ascendancy, and pay homage to an ideology that still shapes the

SHARED GRIEF

In the modern age, preserving heroes has been a particularly left-wing endeavour, particularly at the Communist end of the political spectrum. Some credit this to a desire to put a human face to the struggle against oppression. A less favourable take is that preserving heroes is an act of state control, continuing cults of personality that existed in the heroes' lifetimes, and on a par with the veneration of god-kings in Ancient Egypt.

But there are lessons to learn about the importance of sharing the grieving process. Mourning is never something that is simply 'done'. Loss lingers for a lifetime, and having a platform to express it publicly can be cathartic. Mourners who grieve at Lenin's tomb are paying their respects not only to the founder of the Soviet Union but also to shared experiences, and to many martyrs closer to home who perished in pursuit of a common goal. Ultimately, it's a gesture of solidarity.

Russian worldview three decades after the fall of Communism.

The mechanics of preserving a hero for posterity are complex, involving baths of chemicals such as glycerol, formaldehyde, alcohol and potassium acetate, which are painstakingly applied every two years. Working alongside the preservation team, aestheticians use waxes and plastics to patch holes and hide blemishes, maintaining the illusion that Lenin is lying in a state of restful sleep. In truth, scientists from the so-called Mausoleum Group face a constant battle against the natural processes of decay.

AN EXCLUSIVE CLUB

Lenin is not the only enduring hero of the revolution. In Vietnam, the glassy body of Ho Chi Minh sleeps beneath a transparent

Above: Lenin's Mausoleum at Red Square. Opposite: Kumsusan Memorial Palace of the Sun, home to the tombs of Kim Il Sung and Kim Jong Il.

canopy in a grand mausoleum in the centre of Hanoi. In central Běijīng, mourners queue daily to view the glass sarcophagus containing the embalmed body of Mao Zedong. Two generations of the Kim dynasty lie in state in the Kumsusan Memorial Palace of the Sun in Pyongyang, North Korea, giving literal form to the title 'Eternal Leader'.

Like the incorruptible saints of the Eastern Orthodox church, the leaders who built Communism into an empire spanning over 20.7 million sq km (8 million sq miles) lie preserved not simply as humans, but as representatives of a grand idea. Their preservation is less a gesture of mourning than an act of love — an attempt to keep a particular perspective on life frozen in time, in an ever-changing world. The mummifying pharaohs of Ancient Egypt would be proud.

This enthusiasm for preserving revolutionary heroes didn't die with the fall of the Soviet Union. There were plans to put the former Venezuelan leader Hugo Chávez on public display after his death in 2013, but his body began to decay in the humid Venezuelan climate before embalmers could begin the preservation process. It remains to be seen which world leader will be next to join the ranks of the adoringly embalmed.

HIGH-RISE HOMES FOR THE DEAD

With the human population soaring, cities around the world are turning to columbaria — vertical cemeteries where cremains are filed in neat niches, like pigeonholes for the departed.

Taiwan has a mortality problem. The population of this small island has soared from just six million in 1946 to some 23.6 million today, squeezed into an area smaller than the US states of Maryland and Delaware combined. Space in Taiwan is at a premium, and this equation also applies to the dear departed. With all the cemeteries full to bursting point, Taiwan was left with one option in the search for new mortuary real-estate: looking up.

Today, Taiwan hosts the world's largest vertical cemetery, the prestigious True Dragon Tower — a 20-storey high-rise that will eventually accommodate the funeral urns of 400,000 well-heeled Taiwanese citizens. Niches in this ultra-desirable residence can cost anything from US$6500 to US$33,000, and that's before the lavish costs of a traditional Taiwanese funeral are taken into account.

But money is not the only issue. Taiwanese society is ageing rapidly — one in five Taiwanese will be aged over 65 by 2065 — and space for the deceased is in short supply. The government has embraced high-rise cemeteries as a practical solution to the problem of ensuring dignity in death in one of the most densely populated nations on Earth.

A SKYSCRAPER FOR THE DEAD
Nestled into the hills north of Taipei, True Dragon Tower looks like a temple that has experienced a sudden growth

HONEST MORTALITY

Across the world, morticians strive to hide the production-line nature of the funeral business, but a sense of being rushed through the process to make room for the next set of 'customers' often intrudes. At a columbarium, there's no hiding the fact that death is universal and unremarkable – but considering that mortality is as inescapable as taxes, perhaps there's something to be said for being businesslike about it.

Why not be open about the logistics of dealing with death? Why not share mourning with other people who are going through the same process? Why not make the final resting place a comfortable space for the living to spend time? If you need a focus for remembering the departed, a niche is just as effective as a lavish tomb; and demystifying death is a healthy step towards becoming more comfortable with mortality as an integral part of life.

spurt, with a looming frontage bursting skywards from a complex of pagoda-roofed shrines. There are few windows – occupants don't need them – leaving more space for thousands of cremation urns, hidden behind gleaming porcelain covers.

Looking at the banks of identical niches, you might get a hint of capsule hotel and a whisper of space-age locker room, but the eternal addresses become increasingly lavish as you climb up the levels. Premium residents at this self-styled 'hotel for the dead' are accommodated on the sleek 17th floor, where interiors were designed by Pritzker Prize–winning Japanese architect Tadao Ando.

High-status niches are only part of the picture. The garden surrounding the True Dragon Tower is arranged according to feng shui principles, with its back to the mountains and its frontage facing the Taiwan Strait. Marble stairways cascade down forested slopes. Golden Buddhas beam benevolently. This is a location for reflection and contemplation, not a place that revels in the sadness of death.

Above: Glass Buddha statue niches inside the Ruriden Columbarium in Tokyo. Opposite: The 32-storey Memorial Necrópole Ecumênica in Santos, Brazil.

A MODERN WAY OF GRIEVING

Two-thousand-year-old columbaria have been uncovered in Italy and Israel, but high-rise homes for the dead are now popping up wherever in the world city planners are struggling with the problem of finding graveyard space, from Brazil's 32-storey Memorial Necrópole Ecumênica to Israel's Art-Deco-inspired Yarkon Cemetery.

What marks out vertical cemeteries across the globe is a focus on accommodating mourning within the routines of modern life. Singapore's luxurious Nirvana Memorial Garden offers on-site feng shui consultants, bookable suites for private contemplation and an airy, bamboo-lined cafe; Kuala Lumpur's Nirvana 2 Center even has valet parking.

At the Ruriden Columbarium in Tokyo's Koukokuji Buddhist Temple, it's all about technology. Niches are adorned with rainbow-coloured crystal Buddhas that light up a celestial white when relatives scan a digital keycard. The modern necropolis is not a sombre place to be avoided, but somewhere to drop by on the way home from work to feel close to the departed.

MOURNING

When outpourings OF GRIEF AND displays of REMEMBRANCE ARE STRIPPED AWAY, WHAT REMAINS IS SURPRISINGLY POWERFUL.

DEATH WAILING

Tremulous chanting and guttural cries ring out at funerals from Ireland to Australia. Losing a loved one is beyond description, but through the practice of death wailing, it has a voice.

The sound of death wailing reverberates through your entire body. This vocal accompaniment to mourning is practised around the world, and it can be anywhere on the auditory spectrum, from cries and yelps to husky moaning. But what all death wails have in common is their otherworldly sound, which almost vibrates through the listener.

Across the world, in most cases death wailing is led by a professional mourner, with grieving friends and family joining in the chorus. Over time, the sound becomes almost hypnotic, as mourners lament in unison.

UNIVERSAL SOUNDS OF SORROW

In Uganda, death wailing can be high-pitched and tremulous. Among Aboriginal Australians, death wailing is a low-pitched mourning song, though the deceased's name will never be uttered (page 149). In early China, it was once considered essential to wail so that the deceased's spirit could find its way.

Just as the custom of professional mourners is waning, death wailing, too, has dwindled; in some countries it has almost entirely died out. In many places, though, death wailing continues to give voice to grief.

EXPRESSIONS OF GRIEF

One of the best-known forms of death wailing occurs during Irish funerals, where a *bean chaointe* (keening woman)

SINGING AWAY SADNESS

Through chanting, drumming or playing, music has long been important in funerary rituals. Today, Frank Sinatra's *My Way* has worldwide funeral popularity, thanks to lyrics eulogising an imperfect but satisfying life. One of Mexico's most popular funeral songs is Juan Gabriel's *Amor Eterno* (Love Eternal), a ballad yearning for reunion in the afterlife.

But music's true power transcends lyrics. Grief can be overwhelming, and it rises like waves; this is mirrored by death wailing's unstructured, crescendoing laments. Grief can't be contained within a few orderly verses; likewise, death wails aren't confined to a musical arrangement. They might be atonal, repetitive or devoid of lyrics altogether. This is why death wailing is so cathartic for all who take part: where words fail us, death wailing can bring grief to the surface with its musical outbursts of pure, unrestrained emotion.

performs mourning songs that can crescendo into a chorus of wailing (p13). But there are parallel traditions of female-led death wailing around the world.

In northwestern regions of the Philippines, the Ilocano people chant and sing spontaneously after hearing the news of a death, a practice known as *dung-aw*

(lament). Anyone who hears it may join in, responding to or echoing the words being uttered. The effect is almost viral: sound travels from household to household, with listeners joining the chorus and repeating the lyrics and melodies they hear. In this way, an individual family's grief becomes community grief.

Above: *Ogene* drumming at an African funeral ceremony.
Opposite: Mourners gather at a remembrance ritual in the Philippines.

THE ROLE OF WOMEN

Across cultures where death wailing is practised, women generally take a leading role. Since historic roles assigned to women usually demand public decorum or restraint, death wailing is an interesting exception. Women are able to assert themselves in the public domain by assuming the role of chief mourner or primary vocalist.

One example is the *oppari* tradition of South India, where female relatives of the deceased sing during the funeral ceremony. The practice was once led by paid mourners and is now gradually fading into obscurity in urban areas, partly because the profession is stigmatised; but the custom thrives in rural Tamil Nadu.

Oppari is notable for its unity of sound, usually a trilling, repetitive lament in a minor key. Like *dung-aw* in the Philippines, *oppari* may be improvised by the vocalists, who narrate anecdotes about the deceased's life and mention the relatives as well as loved ones who are present.

As the chanting intensifies, vocalists may strike themselves to the rhythm of a beating drum, in an effort to externalise buried sorrow. This is a powerful symbol of how painful it is to accept a loved one's death, and how necessary it is to surface – and express – feelings of grief.

ISLAMIC FUNERAL CUSTOMS

Even beyond birth and death, Muslims belong to God — so Islamic end-of-life customs reinforce spiritual commitments like modesty, cleanliness and facing the direction of Mecca.

Muslims know the last words they'll ever hear: 'There is no god but God, and Muhammad is the Messenger of God.'

These words are the *shahadah*, the Islamic declaration of faith and one of Islam's five pillars. The *shahadah* permeates the lives of Muslims from the moment of birth, when a father whispers them into a newborn's ear, through daily prayers and right until death, when a dying person utters these words as their final oath. It's perfect symmetry, confirming that Muslims unconditionally surrender to God's will — from birth to death, and beyond.

PURIFICATION RITUALS

When a death is announced, community members gather in prayer, uttering the Salat al-Janazah (funeral prayer), which asks God to pardon the dead person, and all dead believers. The body is buried very soon after death, usually within 24 hours. The emphasis on swift burials can be traced to the Hadith (sayings of the Prophet Muhammad), but many Muslims also believe it's more hygienic and kinder to the family, keeping the painful process of making funeral arrangements short. There's neither a vigil, nor a viewing of the body; Muslim families focus on a prompt, dignified burial, followed by restoration of family order.

Just as Muslims ritually cleanse themselves before prayer, a dead

EQUAL IN DEATH

Whether our lives are mighty or modest, we all meet the same fate: it's a theme that graces art and literature across cultures and time periods. In the ancient Mesopotamian work the *Epic of Gilgamesh*, the hero seeks eternal life but comes to accept death. Medieval European artists depicted the *Danse Macabre*, where princes and paupers alike are danced to their graves. Then there's English Romantic poet Percy Bysshe Shelley, who contemplates the ruins of a once-great but now dead and forgotten king in his 1818 work *Ozymandias*.

Islamic customs formalise our equality in death by rejecting showy funerals and encouraging the simple return of bodies to the earth. When outpourings of grief and colourful displays of remembrance are stripped away, what remains is surprisingly powerful: faith so solid that it eclipses our urge to lament the inevitable, and reminds us not to immortalise our humble, transient lives.

body must also undergo *ghusl al-mayyit* (purification) before burial. The body is washed three times with water, soap and perfume, in as modest a manner as possible. There are strict rules governing who may wash the body, based on age, gender and relationship with the deceased; and the body's modesty is safeguarded, even in death; a cloth is used to shield their private parts during purification. Once it has been cleansed, the body is shrouded in *kafan* (simple cloth) and readied for burial.

RETURNING SIMPLY TO EARTH

Muslims believe in the resurrection of the dead on Judgement Day, so bodies are buried, not cremated, to maintain their physical integrity. Autopsies are discouraged (other than in extreme cases, such as the solving of a crime) and embalming is generally not performed (except where not doing so would contravene a country's laws).

Death is humankind's great equaliser. Bodies are buried simply and usually without a coffin. They're placed on stone

Above: Kozha Akhmed Yassawi Mausoleum, southern Kazakhstan.
Opposite top: Sidi Benachir Cemetery in Salé, Morocco. Bottom: Al-Baqi Cemetery is the first and oldest Islamic cemetery of the ancient holy Islamic city of Medina, in present-day Saudi Arabia.

keep a modest tone. Muslim graves are marked simply and humbly, generally with a low stone marker, based on Hadith that decreed tombs should be low, almost level with the ground but not so flat that they can be accidentally walked on.

Most family members adopt a three-day mourning period, but this rises to 40 for close family members. Widows, meanwhile, undergo *iddah* (a period of waiting), for four months and 10 days. Not only does this codify a period of mourning, it also removes any doubt about the paternity of children if the woman decides to remarry quickly.

EXCEPTIONS TO THE RULE

Islam is an ever-practical religion, so there are exceptions to many rules. For example, the restriction on performing autopsies can be waived when they're required by criminal cases. During times of war, where it isn't possible to follow all Islamic rules, it's deemed practical and permissible to bury bodies on a battlefield. There are even guidelines for how to perform a funeral in space, put together as part of the Malaysian National Space Agency's guidebook for Muslims on interstellar missions.

One grey area is organ donation. For example, the Muslim Law Council in the UK issued an edict allowing organ

or wood lining the bottom of a grave, and positioned facing the direction of Mecca (Islam's holiest city, the birthplace of the Prophet Muhammad). Close family members throw three handfuls of soil into the grave, while speaking a Quranic verse that affirms how we return to the earth we were created from, before gravediggers fill in the rest, watched over by

an eldest son or other leading mourner. Finally, there's a prayer for the forgiveness of the dead that marks the end of the burial ceremony, followed by a gathering where mourners will share memories and a meal.

MODESTY IN MOURNING

There's no outright prohibition on vocal mourning or ostentatious funerals, but Muslims generally donation, where a donation would save a life. Meanwhile in Malaysia, studies have found that most Muslims are in favour of organ donation but still find the topic taboo. Although many Muslims have shied away from this practice, others have pointed to the Quran's words that for someone who saves a life, 'it is as if he saves the lives of all humankind.'

Opposite: The founder of the Samanid dynasty built Ismael Samani Mausoleum in Bukhara, Uzbekistan in the 10th century, to honour his father. Right: The Muslim cemetery in Jerusalem's Old City.

ISLAMIC TOMBS, FROM MODEST TO MARVELLOUS

According to Islamic tradition, tombs should be modest. But there are no rules without flamboyant exceptions: one of the most famous burial sites in the world, the Taj Mahal, is an opulent marble mausoleum built by a Muslim emperor, Shah Jahan, who led India's Mughal Empire to its apogee in the mid-17th century.

The Taj is far from the only extraordinary mausoleum built by Muslims. Ismael Samani Mausoleum in Bukhara, Uzbekistan, is a symmetrical, fortress-like tomb with intricately patterned brickwork and towering arches. In southern Kazakhstan, the blue-domed Mausoleum of Khoja Ahmed Yasawi – the largest of its kind in Central Asia – houses the tomb of a 12th-century Sufi mystic.

Even where Muslims opt for simple grave markers, immense care is devoted to the location of some burial sites. In Kassala, Sudan, archaeologists have discovered medieval Islamic gravesites arranged in spiral patterns, where successive burials radiate out from a single ancestor's grave. Researchers have compared these sites to stars within a galaxy (apt, considering the immense contribution of Muslim thinkers to astronomy). These constellations of graves continue to inspire new thought and perspectives on Islamic history.

LAKOTA SOUL KEEPERS

The Lakota people, whose lands are in America's North and South Dakota, don't die – they 'walk on' to the spirit world, leaving behind an essence that blooms in generations to come.

A *čhaŋnúŋpa* (ceremonial pipe) is carefully passed from hand to hand. Each mourner takes their turn to inhale from the long-stemmed pipe, letting out puffs of smoke that curl up to the heavens.

To many Native American tribes, such as the Lakota people (also known as Teton Sioux), smoke acts as a conduit: it carries the prayers and hopes of the grief-stricken up to the spirit world. Death itself is understood as a transition between worlds.

The Lakota people conceptualise death as 'walking on' – it's a way station that makes up part of a journey, rather than a person's final destination.

DIVERSE GRIEVING RITUALS
Native American cultures are a mosaic of different beliefs and practices. According to the Federal Register, there are no fewer than 574 different tribes within the United States, and each one has unique customs for life milestones, from birth to burial.

Nonetheless, there are common themes in Native American death customs. After a death, mourners may wail, lament and cut off their hair. Certain activities become taboo, like consuming intoxicating substances. Many tribes paint the faces of the dead red, a colour symbolic of life; and it's common to dress the deceased in jewellery, moccasins and a cloak. The community might gather for a night vigil to share stories about the deceased.

AN ETERNAL LEGACY

To the Lakota people, as well as other Native American tribes, dying means stepping out of our physical form and into the spirit world, a realm free from pain and sorrow. This inevitable transition isn't something to fear, but it's still natural for the dead person's family to mourn — and rituals like the Keeping of the Soul give their loss a tangible form.

Guarding a soul bundle soothes the physical and the spiritual feelings of loss that accompany a death. Keeping it for as long as a year allows a gradual period of adjustment before the release of the soul in a cathartic and emotional final ceremony. And by ritually infusing young attendees with the soul's essence, the Lakota people have found a way to formalise our most natural hope: that our lives can have an enduring influence. By ritually transmitting our essence to our descendants, we can live on.

There are practical customs, too. The Lakota moral code assigns a high value to generosity, and so some of the deceased's belongings may be given away.

THE 'SOUL BUNDLE'

The Lakota people typically bury their dead, but the treatment of the soul is considered much more ritually important than what happens to the body. One of the Lakota people's seven sacred rites is Wanáǧi Yuhápi (the Keeping of the Soul), which purifies the soul of the deceased and helps them along their journey to the spirit world.

First, a lock of the dead person's hair is held over burning

Above: Chief Red Cloud, celebrated chief of the Oglala Lakota, one of the seven Lakota subtribes, circa 1900. Opposite: a wild bison surveys South Dakota; an expanse of Wind Cave National Park in South Dakota.

during their periods, and that it might extinguish the power of a ceremony leader performing the last rites.

RELEASING THE SOUL

The soul bundle is considered to be a seed planted in the hearts of the mourners; its influence can live on. A family member will keep the soul bundle for up to a year in a safe place in their home, and promise to lead a pure life until the soul is released.

The Lakota people prize seven sacred values, which the soul keeper is expected to uphold: prayer, truth, humility, compassion, respect, generosity and wisdom. The soul keeper should try to embody these exemplary characteristics, and only utter words appropriate to their auspicious role. Meanwhile, their community will honour them with food and gifts.

When the day comes to release the soul, the bundle is carried outside, where a ceremonial lodge has been prepared for the final ritual. The ground is scattered with sage, a circle is traced on the ground, and the soul bundle is placed in the centre.

Inside the lodge, a willow post to represent the soul is dressed with a cloak and a simple image of a face. The deceased's possessions are arranged nearby, along with an

sweet grass to be purified, then it's wrapped into buckskin to create a 'soul bundle'. The ceremony leader prays to Wakáŋ Táŋka (the Creator) to bestow strength on the mourners, and beseech the soul to infuse its energy into the people present. A ceremonial pipe is lit (often containing čhaŋšáša, an aromatic mix of leaves and bark that produces a mildly narcotic effect) and passed around for the mourners to smoke.

POTENT RITUALS

These ceremonies are healing for friends and family of the deceased, and the shared experience strengthens

community cohesion. But they must be led by an experienced practitioner, to help the community channel their grief and to ensure these ancient rituals are executed correctly. Performing funeral rites incorrectly can bring bad luck; but done right, they bestow long-lasting good fortune on those involved in the ceremony, especially to the family member undertaking the crucial role: the keeper of the soul.

Interestingly, women who are menstruating are considered too powerful to be allowed close to where funerary rituals are conducted. Some believe that women's power grows offering of food at the foot of the post. The soul keeper will clasp the bundle one final time, before the ceremony leader takes the bundle and uses it to touch four young attendees – to pass on the dead's influence to the next generation. This way, a person's death can instil a sense of community duty, and be the impetus for others to live honourable lives.

Opposite: Interior view of a sweat lodge.
Right: Native American earth lodge.

LEARNING ABOUT NATIVE AMERICAN CULTURES

Native American practices are often viewed through a coloniser lens: oversimplified as mystical and close to nature rather than seen as living, evolving rituals. So it's understandable that the Lakota people – and Native Americans of other tribes – are sceptical and defensive of outsiders seeking inspiration in their rituals.

The best way to learn about Native American beliefs about death and life is by listening to Native American voices, and respectfully visiting sites on their land. Historic burial sites show the unbroken line from Native American past to present, and visiting them can be a moving experience. Effigy Mounds National Monument, associated with around 20 present-day tribes, is near Iowa's northeastern border with Wisconsin. It has around 200 hills; some are believed to be burial mounds, others are sculpted into the shape of animals and birds. There's also a prehistoric burial site at Ocmulgee Mounds National Historic Park in Macon, Georgia.

National Museum of the American Indian sites in New York City and Washington, DC showcase objects associated with death rituals, like funerary urns and four-direction symbols, which are associated with the four stages of life: birth, youth, adulthood and death.

MĀORI MOURNING CEREMONIES

Community ties are pulled tight when a Māori person dies. Through night vigils, cleansing rituals and a great feast, the dead's smooth transition into the afterlife is assured.

From welcoming ceremony to final feast, Māori mourning traditions restore spiritual order and reinforce *whakapapa* (identity and ancestry). Known as *tangihanga* (from *tangi*, to lament), these ceremonies date to the 1300s, when indigenous Polynesians first landed their canoes at Aotearoa (New Zealand).

RELEASING THE SPIRIT

Even before a dying person draws their last breath, the preparations can begin. When someone's death is expected, their passage into the next life can be eased by *tuku wairua*, where a healer or priest utters ritual incantations to release the spirit and prevent it from wandering.

After the death, friends and family will announce the news — and anyone in the community who hears it is duty-bound to assist the grieving family, if they can. If a pillar of the community dies, the family might use poetic phrases such as 'the tōtara in the great forest of Tāne has fallen', which refers to the felling of a strong and nourishing tree.

AT THE HEART OF THE COMMUNITY

The family prepares the body so it can be taken to the *wharenui* (a meeting house at the heart of a marae, community gathering place). In the past, Māori people would cover the dead body with oil and red ochre, then position them with their knees tucked and their arms enfolded around their

COMFORT IN CONTINUITY

By situating mourning practices within a communal building, Māori customs link the living to the dead and the dead to their ancestral lands, reinforcing *whakapapa* (identity and ancestry). When people mourn together in the marae, a single death becomes the entire community's loss, which consoles the bereaved and reduces their isolation. After all, the grounds of the marae have been trodden by countless generations, and they will be frequented by many others yet to come.

We want the lives of departed loved ones to be meaningful, and for their memory to long outlast their deaths. We can achieve this by situating their deaths within the reassuring solidity of a family tree, or by mourning them with rituals that have outlived centuries. This way, we can be sure they have made their mark: they are part of an unbroken tradition, a chain that connects the distant past to the present day.

legs, before wrapping them in a cloak. Today, the body might be embalmed and placed in an open casket.

However the body is prepared, the community greets its arrival at the marae with a traditional *pōwhiri* (welcoming ceremony), with the unmistakeable Māori display of ferocity and love that they would extend to any living visitor. The body lies in state for

Above: The coffin of Māori Queen Dame Te Atairangikaahu is carried to her final resting place, the sacred burial ground at Mt Taupiri.
Opposite: *Wharenui* (meeting house) of the Te Arawa tribe, Rotorua.

up to three days before burial, during which Māori mourners arrive wearing black and crowned with wreaths of kawakawa, a medicinal plant with distinctive heart-shaped leaves.

INVIOLABLE MOURNING

As in other Polynesian cultures, Māori people observe the concepts of tapu (taboo – subject to spiritual restriction) and *noa* (a blessing that removes the taboo). After a death, restrictions descend upon the immediate family (tapu), but completing various ceremonies can remove them (*noa*). For example, the *whānau pani* (close family) might remain silent, and they will often refrain from eating for three days of mourning, until rituals are conducted to lift these restrictions.

Mourners who gather at the marae will pray and deliver eulogies that directly address the deceased. There will be tears, but Māori mourners are encouraged to share good, bad and funny memories. The deceased is urged to depart on a 'spirits' journey'; according to some Māori beliefs, the spirits of the dead fly up the coast to the sea-smashed headland of Te Rerenga Wairua

Top: Māori warriors at the *tangihanga* for entertainer Sir Howard Morrison. Middle: *Wharenui* in Waitangi National Reserve. Bottom: The lighthouse at Te Rerenga Wairua, last stop before the underworld.

(Cape Reinga), before descending into the underworld.

In the past, extreme physical expressions of mourning were common, such as *haehae* (ritual self-harm), usually cutting into one's skin with sharp-edged shells. The *whakamomori* (suicide) of widows was also a culturally accepted act of grief.

BURIAL & FEASTING

On the third day, after a final vigil, the coffin is closed and processed to its burial place. Māori burial places were once closely guarded secrets, to ensure the dead's enemies would not dig up their bones. But

after the first European settler cemeteries were founded in the 19th century, Māori people began to establish their own *urupās* (cemeteries) near the marae.

After the burial, mourners wash their hands to ritually cleanse themselves and remove tapu, and the deceased's home and place of death may also be ritually purified with prayers. The final restrictions are lifted with a *hākari* (feast) – a particular relief to mourners who have been abstaining from food. Sharing food is a way to welcome mourners back to the realm of the living, as well as show hospitality to visiting guests. That night,

family and friends are encouraged to recover and rest. Meanwhile, anyone who was unable to attend the funeral might experience the ritual of *kawe mate* (carry the dead), where a photograph of the deceased is brought to them.

Though feasting and 'carrying the dead' are common among modern Māori people, the final rite – reburial – is much less so. In this custom, bones are exhumed after one year to be scraped clean, stained with ochre and reburied. Today, a ceremony to unveil the headstone can act as a stand-in second burial – and an occasion for renewed mourning on the anniversary of the death.

THE GODDESS OF DEATH

Māori mythology entwines birth and death into one powerful creation story. The creator deity Tāne-mahuta is said to have fathered children with his own daughter, Hine-tītama – who did not realise his identity. When Hine-tītama discovered that her lover was also her father, she fled to the realm of the dead and refused to return. She commanded Tāne-mahuta to raise their offspring in the

world of the living, while she would remain below – and draw their children down to the realm of the dead when their time came. From then on, she would be known as Hine-nui-te-pō, the goddess of death.

This myth portrays death as the inevitable counterpart to life: Tāne-mahuta brings new life into the world, while Hine-nui-te-pō ushers it into the next life. Other stories tell of demigods who attempted to bypass death's grim inevitability, to predictably

futile results. Shapeshifting trickster Māui-tikitiki-a-Taranga attempted to enter Hine-nui-te-pō's vagina and come out of her mouth, to reverse the cycle of birth and death and win immortality. Māui-tikitiki-a-Taranga transformed himself into a lizard to attempt this feat while the goddess slept, but Hine-nui-te-pō awakened and crushed the life out of him. There's no cheating the goddess of death.

RITUAL FINGER AMPUTATION

Ritual amputations are a fading custom on the island of New Guinea, but their symbolism is brutally clear. When a mourner cuts off their finger, they personify the community's sorrow and grief's physical toll.

Travellers in remote parts of New Guinea island often marvel at the dexterity with which local women weave baskets from tree bark. Then they double-take, noticing that some women have multiple missing fingers. This is the result of *ikipalin*, ritual finger amputation after a death in the family.

Today, only elderly women carry these ritual scars – the practice has now been banned. But *ikipalin* was once commonplace, especially among the Dani people of Western New Guinea's Central Highlands and Highland Papua, Indonesia.

Even hearing about the practice might force you to take a steadying breath... Finger amputations are performed with the help of family, either using a stone blade or by cinching the digit with rope to cut off circulation before breaking the bone and severing the finger. The wound is cauterised, or healing herbs are used to stem bloodflow. Women may undergo *ikipalin* again and again for each loss, learning to adapt to daily activities, like weaving and cooking with less than half of their fingers.

SYMBOLIC BODILY SACRIFICE

The amputatation of a finger is a metaphor for the effect of a death on a community. The fingers of a hand work in unison, just like a community needs its members to work together. When a death occurs, it creates imbalance – just like a hand

PAIN, MENTAL AND PHYSICAL

Grief is often described as the feeling of losing a limb. It has physical symptoms, like nausea, loss of appetite, fainting and even chronic pain. It's a trauma response that can live in the body and even accelerate ill-health and death. It's understandable, then, that body modification is common among mourners across the world, whether it's ancient and highly ritualised (like *ikipalin*) or more modern, like getting a commemorative tattoo of a loved one's face or name.

Making a permanent alteration to the body symbolically reflects the magnitude of a loss. It manifests the depth of connection between the living and the recently deceased. Though customs like ritual finger amputation are drastic, their symbolism is clear to anyone who has experienced the death of someone close to them. By transforming mental anguish into physical pain, we seek to externalise it. And by doing so, we hope our hearts can heal with our physical wounds.

must relearn its movements after losing a finger.

Removing a finger is thought to restore order by mirroring the community imbalance caused by a death. It's a sacrifice designed to keep malign spirits at bay. In cases of a particularly heavy loss, or the passing of a prominent community member, an ear might be cut off instead.

BODY MODIFICATION IN GLOBAL MOURNING

It's understandable to baulk at a custom that injures an otherwise healthy limb, but the line between body mutilation and modification

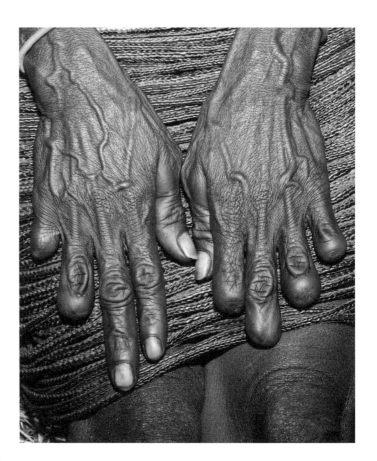

Above: The hands of a Dani woman, Baliem Valley, West Papua. Opposite: A traditional Dani tribal village with *honai* (round houses) and taro fields.

has always been blurred.

Drastic bodily changes have long been a part of mourning conventions, from cutting off hair to tattooing. Like these other modifications, *ikipalin* is not a hasty act intended to demean; it's undergone with a kind of reverence. The amputated finger may even be disposed of in a ritual manner: cremated, with its ashes scattered to the wind.

Finger amputation isn't a custom confined to Western New Guinea and PNG; historically, it may have been more widespread. A 2018 paper published in the *Journal of Paleolithic Archaeology* observes how commonly hands with missing fingers have been depicted on cave walls; the trio of researchers concluded that ritual finger amputation was a very likely cause.

ANCIENT CUSTOMS THROUGH A MODERN LENS

In the case of *ikipalin*, modern observers can't fail to notice that this is a strongly gendered tradition: it has been practised almost entirely by women (and mostly older women). That female bodies are conduits for this extreme show of grief – particularly female bodies past reproductive age – might cause us to question the custom and welcome its disappearance. Nonetheless, *ikipalin's* very brutality expresses powerful truths about grief.

LIFE, DEATH & THE DREAMING IN AUSTRALIA

Aboriginal Australian death customs are diverse and multifaceted, but they all flow from narratives of creation and cosmic connection: from birth to death, we're inextricably linked with our ancestors.

Before creation, the Earth was dark, silent and featureless. Life slumbered, waiting to be awakened – until ancestor beings emerged from the land and sea. These part-animal and part-human demigods travelled across the land creating hills, valleys, rivers, forests – everything found in nature – and setting the stage for humankind's entry.

This is the Dreaming, the origin story and basis for cultural norms among many Aboriginal Australian and Torres Strait Islander peoples. For tens of thousands of years, these hundreds of nations, each with different languages and myths, have inhabited Australia and the islands between Far North Queensland and Papua New Guinea.

There are as many retellings of Dreaming stories as there are nations, but moral codes – and beliefs about life and death – can be traced directly to these powerful narratives and the worldview they establish.

DEATH & THE DREAMING

According to the Dreaming, all life is interconnected and arises from ancestor beings. Spiritual and everyday practices flow from this philosophy; for example, the paths taken by ancestor beings (sometimes referred to as songlines) became a map of Country; not only for trade routes, but for ceremonial purposes.

Life, death and the afterlife are all part of this common tapestry. People's spirits originate from ancestor beings, and after death

ONENESS AFTER DEATH

From birth until death, Aboriginal Australian rituals uphold connectedness to Country and honour rites that date back thousands of years. While the land is our bodies' final resting place, our spirits travel on to take their place among the ancestor beings: death effectively reunites us with our spiritual family.

This makes our lives and deaths rich with meaning. When we're alive, we're part of the natural world's complex fabric, following customs preordained by our ancestors on land sculpted by primordial beings. And when we die, we're sublimated into something immense and immutable, taking our place in a vast cosmic whole.

It's both humbling and awe-inspiring to imagine our final spiritual form as oneness with others. We realise our own insignificance, but we also gain a powerful awareness of the connection between ourselves, our ancestors and our descendants; those who always were, and always will be.

their spirits are taken back into this ancestral whole — just as individual droplets of water can be reabsorbed into a mighty, thunderous river.

THE PAIN OF COLLECTIVE MOURNING

Aboriginal Australian and Torres Strait Islander peoples typically bury or cremate their dead, but there's a vast spectrum of customs to ensure that the deceased person's spirit successfully makes its transition (and doesn't disturb the living).

When a person dies, their community is expected to rally together in mourning (often referred to as 'sorry business') — just as if someone in their own close family had passed away. The family might perform a smoking ceremony, burning

Above: Indigenous performers present the Welcome to Country during a smoking ceremony before the state funeral for activist Uncle Jack Charles.
Opposite top: Aboriginal rock art tells the stories of ancestors and spirits.
Bottom: The Walls of China at Mungo National Park, New South Wales.

Collective mourning and funeral rituals create solidarity within the community, but they can be unbearably painful. Funerals remind Aboriginal Australians of the epidemic of premature death in their communities, which can be linked to the impact of brutal European colonisation, intergenerational trauma and racism. Child suicides, deaths related to alcoholism and dying in police custody are all disproportionately high among Aboriginal Australians. The emotional toll of mourning young lives can lead to communities disconnecting from traditional funeral rites, and fracturing even further.

NAMING THE DEAD

One belief common to many Aboriginal nations is that it's taboo to name the dead. For up to two years after a person's death, their community might avoid saying the deceased's name directly. This restriction is thought to avoid heightening the sadness of grieving relatives, and ensure the dead person's spirit isn't encouraged to linger by the sound of their name. It's also considered more respectful to refer to a dead person with a euphemism or roundabout description.

In modern Australia, this taboo also applies to images and recordings of deceased people.

Above: The Aboriginal Memorial, an installation of 200 hollow log coffins, honours all the Indigenous people who have lost their lives defending their land; National Gallery of Australia, Canberra.

native plants like eucalyptus bark in the home of the dead person to cleanse them and usher their spirit onwards. As a visual symbol of grief, mourners might also daub their faces with white pigment, or cut their own hair.

Watch a documentary or attend a photography exhibition in Australia and you might see a warning that images of the dead are on display.

RITUAL POWER OF RED OCHRE

Over millennia, some death customs have fallen out of use. For example, white-clay mourning caps known as *kopis* were once worn for months after a death, and news of deaths would be passed between communities by symbolic carvings on a talking-stick, which was burned after the message had been relayed.

Before Australia was colonised, it was also common to bury the dead in two phases. First, the dead body would be painted with red ochre, an iron-rich natural pigment that symbolises ancestral blood to many Aboriginal Australians. Next, the body would be wrapped and placed on a raised platform.

After months exposed to the elements, only bones would remain and these would be stained with ochre and transported to a second burial site, perhaps a log coffin. Though this practice is now rare

in Australia, it thrives in other countries, such as Nigeria (see page 49).

When ancient human remains were excavated from Willandra Lakes, a lunar landscape in outback New South Wales, it became clear that ochre's ritual significance was part of a long, unbroken tradition. An ancient hunter-gatherer (dubbed the 'Mungo Man' after the dry lake where he was found) had been buried with his body coated in ochre more than 42,000 years ago — confirming the astonishing longevity of Aboriginal traditions.

HOLLOW LOG COFFINS & BURIAL TREES

Humankind's harmony with nature is a fundamental component of Aboriginal Australians' beliefs, and trees have played important roles in burial rites. In northern Australia, it was once common to create log coffins by sculpting tree trunks and decorating them with colourful patterns and symbols. These cylindrical ossuaries, sealed up with a wooden lid, were the final resting places of ochre-stained bones. Nowadays, hollow-log coffins are rarely used to house bones, but the art of sculpting hollowed-out tree trunks and decorating them with elaborate designs has endured. Swing by the National Gallery of Australia in capital city Canberra to see a forest of these beautiful columns on display.

In New South Wales, especially among the Gamilaroi and Wiradjuri peoples, living trees were used as burial sites for prominent community members.

Only a very particular type of tree suited this role: an old-growth tree with a natural hollow large enough for remains to be placed inside. Community members would carve geometric patterns like circles and chevrons into the bark, as a blueprint for the deceased's path to the spirit world and to mark the tree as a site of ritual significance. The markings also warn passersby that they are approaching sacred ground.

JEWISH MOURNING AROUND THE WORLD

For millennia, Jewish customs have extended respect to the living and the dead. These diverse traditions guide mourners from the moment of a death right through to anniversaries and prayerful remembrance.

One of the largest Jewish burial grounds in Europe can be found in Prague's Jewish Cemetery. As you walk through the cemetery's tangled weeds, you see granite headstones dating right back to the 15th century. Stooping low to examine the moss-covered lettering more closely, you notice a small heap of pebbles, carefully placed on the top of the headstone: a Jewish mourning custom that dates back thousands of years.

Jewish culture is a kaleidoscope, and its death customs have been touched by influences from across Europe, Africa, the Americas and beyond – everywhere the Jewish diaspora have built their communities. But despite the passage of time and multiple cultural influences, Jewish death customs have a clear through-line: an orderly burial and mourning process, with codes and customs designed to maximise the dignity of the deceased and their family.

MOURNERS IN BETWEEN

According to Jewish customs, there are clear roles after a death. During the period of *aninut* (between the death being announced and the burial), immediate relatives have the duty to attend to the practicalities of the funeral.

Close relatives like parents, children, spouses or siblings are considered to occupy a state outside usual life: they are *onen* (between). They might tear their clothing in grief, and the

LET GRIEF BREATHE

Jewish customs exhibit a deep understanding of how sorrow can affect a family, and how lingering it can be. During the initial aninut period, anyone outside the close family is encouraged to help with practical preparations, and not to expect the close family to socialise or interact. Though burials are swift and the initial mourning period is confined to a month, it's understood that close relatives require a much longer mourning period, in the form of uttering the Mourner's Kaddish for 11 months.

These rituals and duties also affirm the dignity of every member of the community. All people are considered equals before God, so people with no family to inter them – including those outside the community, and criminals – are also given burials. Not only is this *chesed shel emet* (the greatest kindness), it reminds the community to be humble and extend care to all.

location of the tear reflects their relationship with the deceased: for example, over the heart for a parent, or on the right-hand side for a sibling.

A SWIFT, DIGNIFIED BURIAL

Respect for the dead is paramount, and washing and preparing a body for burial is considered to be *chesed shel emet*: the greatest of kindnesses which cannot be repaid. Respect and care for the dead also includes burying the body as soon as possible, to usher along their journey out of this life.

But Jewish death customs also uphold hygiene. Not only are burials swift, but they must take place a distance away from where people live. Jewish customs also encourage people to wash their hands after sitting with the

Above: Jerusalem's Jewish Cemetery overlooks the city from the Mount of Olives. Opposite top: A funeral procession in Crown Heights, Brooklyn. Bottom left: Jewish tombs, Jerusalem. Bottom right: A kosher candle burns for Yom Kippur, Plzeň, Czech Republic.

body, and after returning from the burial ceremony. Cremation, on the other hand, is rare in Jewish communities, as it is considered an act of destruction on the body.

After a brief funeral service, the body is carried to the grave in seven stages, with a symbolic pause between each one, often accompanied by a recitation of Psalm 91 – a soul-stirring affirmation that God is a refuge and fortress. Some Jewish communities in Europe orient the body so that the head is symbolically facing Jerusalem. When the casket is lowered, mourners throw earth into the grave. In the past, this was done by hand, though in modern ceremonies people may use the less-effective backside of a shovel – to show their reluctance to see their loved one depart.

SITTING SHIVA
Once the body is buried, the week-long period of shiva (mourning; literally 'seven') begins – only pausing for Shabbat (the Sabbath, between sundown on Friday and Saturday).

People may gather in a single place for shiva, or across multiple locations (perhaps different family homes). A large memorial candle will be lit, and kept burning throughout the week. It's common to serve food symbolic of life and renewal, like eggs, and for religious services to take place – with frequent utterance of the

Mourner's Kaddish, a prayer for abundant peace.

Throughout shiva, certain activities are forbidden – haircuts, washing, doing laundry. Mourners are encouraged to focus on mourning rather than their own appearance, and mirrors may be covered for the same reason.

Some constraints are lifted after the weeklong shiva. Laundry and grooming can resume, but festivals, live music and other public entertainment are frowned on until *shloshim* (one month) has passed. Though this concludes the official mourning period for most of the family, it's customary for people mourning a parent or spouse to recite the Mourner's Kaddish for a full 11 months. There will also be a separate, brief ceremony for the unveiling of the headstone, with readings and the Mourner's Kaddish.

REMEMBRANCE OVER TIME
When visiting a grave, many Jewish people lay small pebbles on top of the headstone instead of flowers. The origins of this ancient custom are lost in time; they might date to desert burials (with piles of stones serving as a simple grave marker) or represent the rubble of Jerusalem's Second Temple, destroyed by the Romans in 70 CE. Another theory is that they are a simple way to beseech God to bind the soul of the dead into eternal life. Leaving pebbles on top of a grave is a small kindness, whether you know the deceased or not.

Opposite: Tombs and higgledy-piggledy headstones in the Old Jewish Cemetery in Prague, Czech Republic.

SEE IT FOR YOURSELF

You can encounter Jewish death customs by visiting historic cemeteries around the world. Ancient inscriptions and states of upkeep teach us a great deal about global Jewish life.

On a cypress-clad hill east of Jerusalem's Old City is Mount of Olives Cemetery, the holiest of all Jewish burial sites. It holds as many as 150,000 graves – scholars, politicians and luminaries, along with people who died in the 1948 Arab–Israeli War. The cemetery's proximity to Temple Mount, where the resurrection of the dead is believed will take place, makes it an especially auspicious burial spot.

The oldest Jewish cemetery in the US is in New York's Lower Manhattan, where the pocket-sized First Shearith Israel Graveyard tells of the first Spanish and Portuguese Jews who established a community here. In Europe, the oldest surviving Jewish cemetery is Heiliger Sand in Worms, Germany. Dating back to the 11th century, it suffered greatly from 17th-century vandalism, but Jewish people continued to be buried here until 1940. Tragically, many historic Jewish cemeteries have been left unmaintained and have been reclaimed by nature, such as the overgrown Jewish cemetery in Chișinău, Moldova, and the windblown coastal cemetery in Asilah, Morocco.

THE PEOPLE PAID TO WEEP

Weeping, howling and beating their chests, these lamenting women can be found at funerals around the world – and as professional mourners, they're paid by the hour.

All eyes are riveted on a small group of women standing in the church, right next to the open coffin. From their lacy shawls to their tattered shoes, they're all dressed entirely in black. They sway gently in unison, wiping away tears and emitting anguished cries of grief. But these women aren't the close friends and relatives of the deceased: they've never even met. Welcome to the remarkable vocation of paid mourning.

THE OLDEST PROFESSION?
References to paid mourning go back thousands of years. The Christian Bible's Old Testament has numerous references to lamentation as a paid art form – like Jeremiah 9:17-18, which summons the most skilful wailing women. English poet Chaucer also described mourning pageantry, with black-clad women beating their chests to mourn noble deaths.

Paid mourning also transcends geographical boundaries. In ancient China, actors would lead theatrical performances of a person's life at their funeral, and performative mourning became a natural extension of this custom. Meanwhile, in Egypt, professional mourners acted as stand-ins for the goddesses Isis and Nephthys, who were associated with death, darkness and funerals.

In most traditions, it's women who take on this emotionally demanding profession. This is often because of rigid gender stereotypes that women

A RELEASE VALVE FOR GRIEF

However deep our well of grief, it can still be difficult to draw from. At the same time, it can feel vital that other people see our grief, and so understand how deeply loved the deceased was. This is the paradox that professional mourners can resolve: they fulfil our need to express grief, even if we're incapable of doing so ourselves.

Professional mourners also help to open the floodgates for everyone else at a funeral service to unleash their grief. Through their own loud, dramatic cries, professional mourners take centre stage. They give permission for everyone present to free their emotions without feeling self-conscious – no one needs to feel chained by societal expectations.

Even in cultures without professional mourners, there are other ways we can give ourselves permission to grieve fully and authentically, like cultivating a safe and private space to talk, weep and process our sorrows how ever feels right for us.

can express their emotions unguardedly – unlike men, whose reserve and strength are seen as their social currency.

Paid mourning has typically involved noisy spectacles, but sometimes a sombre silence is more fitting. In Victorian England, mourners were simply hired to give the impression of a well-attended funeral.

CUSTOMISED CRYING

Paid mourning is much less common today, but people are still commissioned to cry around the world. China and Egypt each have modern incarnations of their ancient traditions. Over in Greece, professional mourners also play the role of funeral directors; they wash and shroud the body, light candles and ululate sonorously.

In Ghana, some enterprising widows even accept requests for particular styles of crying, from subdued sobbing to dropping to the ground in spasms of grief. Sometimes

Above: Professional mourners at a funeral near Accra, Ghana. Opposite: A team of 'funeral weepers' in China dress in traditional white costumes and paint their faces with red eye make-up to emphasise their tears.

this is a sign of respect to the deceased, but at other times this vocal mourning acts as a spur to elicit more sympathetic donations and gifts to the family, which helps allay the high costs of Ghanaian funerary traditions (page 87).

India's professional mourners offer a similarly physical service. Known as *rudaalis*, these veiled mourners cry, and even strike their chests, for sums of money and sometimes food. *Rudaalis*

are often lower-caste women acting as surrogate mourners for upper-caste women, whose status doesn't permit them expressions of grief.

MOURNING: WOMEN'S WORK

Any profession that commercialises physical or emotional services is taboo, and that goes doubly in the death business. Many women have been stigmatised for performing this role, and it's noteworthy that

India's *rudaalis* are lower-caste women, and that in Ghana and Greece the practice is usually done by widows.

It's hard to escape the way that economic circumstances and gender stereotypes position women as society's grief-carriers. But the existence of professional mourners communicates an important truth: throughout time, our sorrows have yearned for a voice that we aren't always able to give them ourselves.

IMMORTAL ICONS
Symbols of Death & Rebirth

Grinning skulls, creepy bats and jet-black ravens in one corner; pristine lilies, fiery salamander and freshly hatched butterflies in the other – death and rebirth form opposing symbolic armies (with some notable exceptions).

Cultures throughout history have endeavoured to express their deepest mysteries and greatest fears in the emotional shorthand of imagery. The great unknown of death is portrayed with dark and forbidding signs, the optimism of reincarnation in purity and beauty. Other ancient symbols both encompass and surpass notions of death and rebirth, beginning and end – such as the Ancient Egyptian ouroboros, the image of a snake eating its own tail, representing endless return, immortality and the eternal cycle of time.

In each of these symbols we may find a glint of emotional truth, even a glimmer of inspiration. From the philosophical complexity of the Tibetan Buddhist Wheel of Life to the grimly vaudeville antics of the Grim Reaper, the emblems we've created to express and contemplate death and rebirth are pictures worth many thousands of words.

Right: an ancient Egyptian temple wall carving shows goddess Hathor putting the sacred ankh to the mouth of Pharaoh Seti I.

The Ankh

It's commonly known as the 'key of life' – so why is it so often found prominently adorning Ancient Egyptian tombs? In tomb paintings and inscriptions, deities are seen placing the ankh against the lips of the deceased, carrying the breath of life to revive the soul into its new life after death.

For the Ancient Egyptians, the relationship between life and death was fluid. Their afterlife, the Field of Reeds (Aaru), was a perfect reflection of the life one had lived on Earth. Death was simply another stage of life, just as meaningful, and the ankh provided the key to the gates of death and what lay beyond.

This meaning-laden token can simultaneously symbolise life, death, immortality, the natural cycle of the sun and the original act of creation, because, for the Egyptians, all these things were fundamentally linked. Just as the sun sets and then rises, death merely precedes the dawn of a new day.

Above: An ankh in the hand of a god on the wall of a temple near Luxor, Egypt.

SEPVLTVRE

The Winged Hourglass

Sand clocks have a mysterious, untraceable history thought to reach back to Egyptian times. By the Middle Ages they had probably become the most popular way to measure the passing of time – only to be sidelined by the invention of the mechanical clock. But never mind: they found a new, grimly symbolic role. Dutch Renaissance painters revived the hourglass as the star of a new genre of painting, vanitas: metaphorical still-lifes offering viewers a moral meditation on the fleeting nature of existence. A grinning skull, a wilting flower, an extinguished candle and an hourglass, its sands ineluctably running out.

With the addition of a pair of wings, the hourglass became one of the graveyard's most common emblems, a visual pun on the truism we can date back to Roman poet Virgil – *'tempus fugit'* ('time flies'). Its message to the living is clear: your time here is brief, so seize the day.

Above: The winged hourglass appears on a family crypt in Père Lachaise Cemetery, Paris, France.

The Wheel of Life

Reliably found on the outside walls of Tibetan Buddhist temples and monasteries, the Wheel of Life (*Bhavacakra*) represents the basic concepts of Buddhism – birth, death and rebirth – in pictures, intended to describe and teach this profound philosophy of life to the illiterate.

Holding the wheel is Yama, the Lord of Death. Despite his fearsome title and fanged appearance, he is not evil – he reminds us that everything is impermanent, and death is inevitable. Inside the wheel are the Six Realms, which can be understood as forms of existence or states of mind into which people are born according to their *karma*. In the middle, the three causes of all suffering: greed, ignorance and hatred. In the top right corner, outside the wheel to show that he has escaped the cycle of life and death, Buddha points the way, representing hope for the liberation of *nirvana*.

The Phoenix

Perhaps our most ancient and enduring symbol of rebirth, the phoenix is a mythical bird that regenerates itself from its ashes. While the first sighting dates to Greek literature from the 8th century BCE, its origins are disputed – there are some who believe it came from Ancient Egypt. Its connection with the sun – ancient depictions sometimes show it with a halo – lend weight to this theory.

Whatever its origins, the immortal bird rising untouched from the cinders of its fiery end has analogues in many other cultures: the Hindu garuda, the Russian firebird (*zhar-ptitsa*) and the Persian *simorgh*. The phoenix has inspired writers from Dante and Shakespeare to JK Rowling – Fawkes, the pet phoenix of Dumbledore in Rowling's *Harry Potter* series, has introduced the creature to a new generation.

Opposite: A painting of the Buddhist Wheel of Life at the temple in the Punakha Dzong, Bhutan. **Above:** The phoenix is a figure of myth and fantasy.

The Grim Reaper

The Western world's best-known psychopomp (any creature that guides departed souls to the afterlife) the black-cloaked, scythe-wielding Grim Reaper is certainly not the only or the first. In Greek mythology, ferryman Charon helped souls across the river Styx; Norse Valkyries were flying female figures who chose which soldiers would die, then led them to Valhalla. Azrael, the Islamic angel of death, puts the Reaper in the shade with his 4000 wings and body formed by as many eyes and tongues as there are living human beings.

The Grim Reaper emerged into a 14th-century Europe ravaged by the Black Death plague, which remains the world's most fatal pandemic. The vision of death as an animated skeleton represents the fear of a disease that seemed to be spread from others: friends, family, neighbours (it was, in fact, rat fleas). His scythe, a common harvesting tool of the time, speaks chillingly to the scale of the death toll: somewhere between 75-million and 200-million people were mown down – reaped – by the plague.

The Grim Reaper, the Western world's favourite psychopomp.

OFFERING

It's humbling TO ACCEPT THAT our lives & DEATHS ARE MERE SPECKS IN THE UNIVERSE'S VAST DRAMA.

ZOROASTRIAN TOWERS OF SILENCE

Being consumed by birds might sound like an extreme way to exit the material world, but for India's Zoroastrians, it's the natural pathway to the next existence.

Dating back at least 3000 years, Zoroastrianism was old when Christianity and Islam were young, but its followers were scattered across the globe by conflict and persecution. Today, just 25,000 Zoroastrians live In Iran, the religion's birthplace, while the largest stronghold for this ancient faith is the Indian city of Mumbai.

Taking their name from an ancient Indian term for Persians, Mumbai's Parsis have left a powerful stamp on the city, thanks to their entrepreneurial zeal, their Iranian-influenced cuisine and their dakhmas (towers of silence), or, where the bodies of their dead are laid out to be picked clean by vultures.

According to the teachings of the prophet Zarathustra (Zoroaster), dead bodies are *nasu* (unclean) and a magnet for evil spirits. To avoid the contamination of earth, air, fire and water, the dead are ritually washed and swiftly returned to nature, leaving the world as they came into it —

naked and unembalmed.

There are strict taboos about contact with the dead. Only *nasa-salar* (pallbearers) may enter the dakhma, so mourners say their last goodbyes outside the walls. For the final stage of the journey to the afterlife, the dead truly are left in silence.

A VANISHING TRADITION

The preparation of the body for this unusual form of excarnation involves complex purification rituals to guide the soul across the

FUNERALS WITHOUT THE FOOTPRINT

In Zoroastrian death rituals, the forces of evil that enter the body after death are a powerful metaphor for the process of decay, which has the power to cause real harm to the living. But the most notable contrast to Western traditions is the way in which the dead are returned to nature in the most natural state possible.

Considering the effect we have on the natural world in life, there's much to be said for minimising our impact in death. A single human cremation produces as much carbon dioxide as an 800km (500-mile) car journey, while embalming fluid – a noxious mix of formaldehyde, alcohol and other chemicals – has been linked to toxic groundwater pollution near cemeteries.

In contrast, excarnation is almost carbon neutral. Rather than trying to delay the process of decay, perhaps we should be accelerating it, so as to leave as small a carbon footprint on our way out of the world as we made coming into it?

Chinvat Bridge – the link between this world and the afterlife – with ceremonies that continue long after the body has been stripped to bare bones.

"While the dead body is swiftly disposed of, rites for the immortal soul are complex and prolonged, to aid and connect to the immortal soul after death," explains Professor Almut Hintze of the Shapoorji Pallonji Institute of Zoroastrian Studies. "Ceremonies on behalf of the departed are celebrated daily until the 10th day and then again on the 20th day after death, the first anniversary day, and annually for 30 years or roughly a generation."

Or at least, this used to be the custom. In Iran, dakhma funerals were banned by the

Above: Indian vultures, Rajasthan. Opposite: Towers of Silence on the outskirts of Yazd, Iran.

Islamic government in the 1970s and replaced by special stone- or concrete-lined graves to satisfy the taboo on ritual pollution. Today, Mumbai is one of the last places on Earth where Zoroastrian funerals still take place in the traditional way.

SALVATION VIA THE SUN?
Even in India, however, the practice faces an uncertain future. Vulture numbers have plummeted due to urbanisation and the veterinary medicine Diclofenac, which is beneficial to cattle but deadly to vultures. There may no longer be enough carrion feeders left to purify the city's dead.

Dakhma attendants have had to come up with creative solutions. In Mumbai, the Towers of Silence at Doongerwadi use solar concentrators to desiccate bodies, speeding up the process of excarnation while still staying true to Zoroastrian principles of ritual purity.

Working dakhmas are screened from public view, but the ancient hilltop tower at Yazd in Iran is open to visitors. Here you can catch a fascinating glimpse of this ancient practice – from the funerary plinth with its concentric rings for men, women and children, to the central ossuary pit, where bones were stored after being picked clean.

BALI'S CREMATION CEREMONIES

Balinese Hindus free souls from their earthly bonds in elaborate cremation rituals — unforgettable spectacles that immolate the dead within huge, richly decorated bamboo towers, set ablaze and reduced to ash.

Soaring bamboo towers, lavishly decorated in myriad colours and heavily accented with gold, are paraded through the streets of Bali to the hypnotic strains of gamelan music. Sharply dressed in brilliant white with rainbow-coloured accents, processions of mourners follow until the tower reaches a sacred site. Here, the entire creation is set alight in a column of flame that consumes everything, including the remains of the deceased held within.

It's the climactic moment of Ngaben. This Balinese Hindu cremation ceremony forms just part of a set of complex rituals to free the soul from earthly ties and ensure a serene afterlife.

NO-EXPENSE-SPARED CEREMONIES

Ngaben varies greatly around the island of Bali according to a person's status in life, and to family and community customs. One family's tradition will be to cremate bodies individually soon after death; in a neighbouring village, large group cremations will be held once a decade for the dead of all local families.

Expense is always a factor. Even a 'small' ceremony for one person (which will still look lavish to an outsider) costs upwards of US$1300 — a significant amount in a place where the average monthly income is US$150. People with higher community status may merit more elaborate ceremonies, costing over US$6700. Most extravagant

FREEING THE SPIRIT

Celebrating the soul as opposed to mourning a loss is at the heart of Balinese Hindu death ceremonies. Finding your place among the spirits of ancestors is the ultimate reward for a life well lived, and every step of Ngaben is designed to ease this journey and ensure its successful completion.

This focus on the wellbeing of the soul infuses Balinese attitudes to death with optimism. Yet the consequences of life choices are not forgotten. Karma – the sum of one's earthly actions – is the ultimate judge of behaviour. Living a good life ensures good karma, but it's possible to make amends for misdeeds. Eternal damnation has no place in Balinese beliefs, as even those who die with bad karma can get a reprieve through the actions of their descendants. Giving souls a serene afterlife brings joy to both individuals and entire communities – and this is at the heart of the immense effort and dedication required for Ngaben.

of all are the royal cremations for the island's princes and princesses. Months, if not years, of preparation culminate in a seemingly endless procession, with thousands of people and a palatial cremation tower built so high that overhead electrical lines are removed to ensure a clear journey along the streets.

TIME IS OF THE ESSENCE

But whether the Ngaben is large or small, the ceremony must take place on an auspicious date. Priests will look for just the right day amid the plethora of existing ceremonies in Bali's busy sacred calendar.

Costs also play a role in the timing: families that want to

cremate their dead as soon as possible may still have to wait months, or even years, to save the money they'll need to do Ngaben right. If the ceremony cannot take place quickly, families will temporarily bury their dead, later exhuming them for their grand cremation.

BREAKING EARTHLY TIES

Freeing the soul from the body is the heart of Ngaben. One day prior to cremation, the process often begins with a ritual in which priests – alongside four to six people from the immediate community, all younger than the deceased – walk in an anticlockwise circle around and even under the body, in order to

Above: Cremation ceremony in Carangsari Village. Opposite: Villagers join the procession with parasols and banners.

SEE IT FOR YOURSELF

Like so many aspects of daily and sacred life on Bali, Ngaben ceremonies are open to visitors. Those showing proper respect and reverence will be welcome to the crowd of mourners witnessing the release of a soul from earthly ties.

If you're visiting the island for a few weeks or more, you'll have a good chance of witnessing a cremation ceremony. Ask around – as major events within the close-knit island communities, Ngaben are widely known about and scheduled well in advance. Your odds are best if you're staying in or around Ubud, as the region has many sacred sites used for cremations.

The most important consideration is respect. Although this may seem obvious, in recent years inappropriate behaviour by tourists has begun to sour traditional Balinese openness and hospitality. Stay unobtrusive and respectful and you will be tolerated, and even welcomed.

You don't need special dress if you stay on the periphery, but the same clothes required to visit many temples (a sash and sarong) will allow you to mix more easily. There is no problem with taking photographs, as long as you're respectful and discreet, acting with consideration of the solemnity of the occasion.

more demanding by the fact that they frequently spin the tower to further promote the souls' release.

Just before cremation, the body is placed in a casket within the *bade* that's shaped like a cow, elephant, lion or deer. The species depends on the person's status, with a bull being reserved for those of high rank. The highly combustible tower is then set ablaze, with flames shooting skyward. Mourners and visitors alike stand back in mute wonder.

THE RETURN TO NATURE
After the ceremony, the family of the dead carry the ashes to a river or the sea to return them to nature. Three to 12 days later, they return to symbolically 'collect' the spirit and bring it to the family temple, a place of honour where offerings are made to ancestors.

The importance of a successful Ngaben cannot be overstated. Souls not fully liberated are thought to wander the island, stuck between life and afterlife. The Balinese fear these lost souls and attribute misfortunes from missing valuables to crop failure to them. Regular purification ceremonies are held to help these wayward souls complete their journey to the beyond.

sever it from the attachment of earthly things. Mourners then join in the first of several celebratory feasts. Bali's tropical bounty is on opulent display in a riot of colours and enticing aromas: pyramids of oranges, mangoes, bananas, guavas and passionfruit surround roasted suckling pigs and elaborate rice-based dishes.

SET FREE IN FLAMES
The flamboyant tower, or *bade*, is the centre of every Ngaben. Reaching 20m (66ft) or more in height, each *bade* embodies elements representing Bali's spiritual universe. Turtles and dragons at the base symbolise the underworld; above, decorative details in rich colours depict Bali's physical reality, from sea to forests to sacred volcanoes. Crowning the top is a *meru*, a small pagoda-shaped ornament that symbolises heaven.

The route to the cremation site can be long, and dozens of men are required to carry the great weight of the *bade*, a task made

Above top: A seawater Ngaben ceremony on the island of Nusa Penida. Bottom: Grand procession for a royal cremation ceremony in Gianyar.

DEATH & THE OCEAN OF LIFE

*Sang Ketut Rai Wibawa lives in Bangli, in Bali's lush centre,
known for its rivers, temples and rice terraces.*

When I was 17, I was taking care of my father who had been sick for months. He had a lot of pain and suffering, and I said to him: "If you want to go, let go, instead of suffering." When he died, the bathing ritual was not available for him, due to a conflict in ceremonies. He was buried immediately. The priest just poured holy water through a bamboo pipe into the ground to symbolise the bathing ceremony. I had no particular feelings right then, but that changed as the ceremonies reminded me of our obligations on this planet and brought memories of what my father taught me about the positive ways to go through life.

The rituals symbolise that, regardless of differences of clan or culture, we all go to the same ocean, to the same place. This is why we must learn to allow a dying person to 'let go'. There are always a lot of people at death ceremonies, especially cremations. For me this shows how we are never alone, but always helping each other in the same ocean of life.

"My feelings for death have evolved as I have aged and learned, both from those that came before me and through my own experiences. My emotions were much different when I was a child. When there was a death and they would begin the ceremonies in our family compound, I felt sadness, though I did not cry. But the cremations could be scary, and I was afraid. Bodies may have been buried for years, so I did not understand the connection. I'd wonder what was going on.

END-OF-LIFE DOULAS

Birth and death are the only truly universal experiences. But though midwives accompany our journeys into the world, there's often no one to guide us out — unless you hire an end-of-life doula.

With deep reserves of compassion and calm, end-of-life doulas are devoted to easing the transition from this life to the next. Though the concept is relatively new to many Western cultures, there are echoes of this practice throughout history, where community leaders have played ceremonial or practical roles in attending to the dying.

The term doula comes from the ancient Greek 'serving woman'. As with birth doulas, end-of-life doulas are hired for emotional and practical support: ensuring the dying person is never alone, providing a listening ear, and being an advocate when they are unable to speak for themselves — voicing deathbed preferences for painkillers, or a priest.

STEWARDS OF DEATH

Many end-of-life doulas embark on this path because of their own losses; having seen their loved ones die, it becomes clear how meaningful end-of-life work can be. It's as much a vocation as a profession: intimate, intense, and as transformational for the doula as for the dying person.

FREEING FAMILIES FROM FEAR

End-of-life doulas also educate the dying person and their family about the physical processes that accompany death, to reduce fear or confusion when they arrive. Dying people can become restless, or experience illusions or auditory hallucinations. They might become highly lucid or

SPIRITUAL CAREGIVING

Death can never be fully knowable, even with the strongest convictions in science, religion – or both. It's the mysterious state from which none report back, the shared destiny of every human on the planet. Given the universality of death's great unknown, it's remarkable that so many cultures don't consistently cater to the emotional, spiritual and philosophical needs of the dying.

Not everyone will be aware when their own death is approaching. But for those of us who are, it's daunting to face the void alone. Whether through an end-of-life doula, support group or the help of trusted friends, we can use our remaining time to contemplate our transition. We can reflect on monumental questions about the meaning of our life, and the legacy we leave behind. Not only does this introspection comfort us in our remaining days, it's an impetus for those who join us in this process to reflect on their own lives.

speak about going on a journey. These stages of the dying process can be frightening, but an end-of-life doula has the skills and knowledge to reassure and advise the person.

Their services might span a few days, in the case of a rapid illness, or even years if there's a terminal diagnosis. In these situations, an end-of-life doula can assist with documenting memories and wrapping up unfinished business. But a doula's work doesn't end at the moment of death: they often continue their relationship with relatives through follow-ups, helping to console the grieving and usher them through the mourning process.

Above and opposite: End-of-life doulas offer emotional and physical support to those nearing life's final destination, and their families.

HOW TO BECOME AN END-OF-LIFE DOULA

End-of-life care is evolving fast, and doulas are no exception. In Europe and the US, end-of-life doulas began as complements to the medical and emotional aid delivered by hospice workers, particularly during the natural-death movement that began in the 1970s and '80s. Nowadays, not only do end-of-life doulas help with practical tasks like arranging respite care for carers or summoning relatives when death is near, they also facilitate a dying person's reflections. They increasingly offer specialist services based on faith or type of death, and their role now includes spiritual and philosophical counselling.

How do you know if you're suited to this path? You should be a good listener, discreet and nonjudgmental, and knowledgeable about rituals across religions and cultures.

Education and coaching are available through the International End-of-Life Doula Association. In the US, the University of Vermont offers a professional certificate; the programme, which has had 3000 graduates at the time of writing, received a surge of interest during the COVID-19 pandemic. Faced with death on an enormous scale, many of us contemplated what it means to have a 'good death' – and how to make this accessible to everyone.

SWEDISH DEATH CLEANING

Spare your heirs the burden of your belongings. Through Sweden's art of 'death cleaning' you'll relish a joyful and clutter-free life, and your loved ones will avoid an almighty clean-up when you're gone.

" just can't bear to part with them." With these helpless words, we consign shoeboxes of mementoes, stacks of books and cumbersome old furniture to the forgotten corners of our minds and our homes. We'll deal with the clutter one day, we reason; but for many of us, the day never comes. Instead, mountains of our belongings will become someone else's decision to make – probably one of our descendants, who is bequeathed the unhappy task of clearing out our home when we die.

Sorting through a deceased relative's belongings is an overwhelming task. When you're freshly grieving, poring over a loved one's possessions can set off new agonies. You'll encounter items that remind you of them, or photographs that unearth a side of them you never knew. Through a mist of tears, you're forced to make snap decisions about keeping, donating or discarding their beloved knick-knacks.

SENTIMENTALITY BEGONE

Gothenburg-born artist and author Margareta Magnusson experienced this gruelling process multiple times, and decided there had to be a better way. Magnusson wrote a book that introduced the world to *döstädning* (literally, 'death cleaning'), and sparked a revolution of middle-aged women and men seeking a simpler, more orderly life.

Magnusson, a champion of exuberant ageing and the art

A LIGHTER LIFE WELL–LIVED

When you die, it's the end for you, but not for your family. Anything you leave behind becomes their business (and their problem), whether it's a wardrobe stuffed with moth-eaten coats, folders of dog-eared paperwork or a box full of the 'good china'. Death cleaning challenges us to relieve loved ones from dealing with our belongings when we die.

As we age, many of us are instinctively drawn toward death cleaning: have you ever helped older relatives haul bags of trinkets to a charity shop? But the urge to cling onto our belongings is even more powerful. After all, we've spent a lifetime accumulating them. Reversing that process requires us to accept that life is growing shorter.

By framing death cleaning as a clarifying process, you'll experience its fullest benefits. It isn't giving up or choosing to fade away: it's unburdening yourself of what you don't need anymore, to live your richest life.

of the good death, offers her readers a clear message: if you can't think of anyone who will be happier for you keeping something (including you), then don't. In her 2017 book *The Gentle Art of Swedish Death Cleaning*, Magnusson urges us to temper sentimentality about our cherished belongings with practical considerations. Agonising over what to do with Mum's masses of books or Dad's collection of antique teapots is a practical problem — one you can easily spare your family by periodically and mindfully sorting through your belongings.

A MAGICAL MINDSET SHIFT

Though it's called 'death cleaning', the practice doesn't need to be undertaken when you're at death's door; it's a process, rather than dramatically clearing the decks. Start in your mid-60s, recommends Magnusson, while you're still fit and well enough for the task of unburdening those bookcases. Begin with anything

out of sight, like boxes that you've pushed under beds or stored in an attic. Digitally declutter by going through and unsubscribing from services, and closing old email or unused social media accounts. Leave souvenirs and letters until last, as they're difficult to part with.

The process doesn't need to be dreary. It's an excuse to pick up a photo album, hold ornaments in your hands, and leaf through a once-loved book. Enjoy and appreciate the trove of objects you've gathered, and revive old memories. You can even involve your loved ones in death cleaning; poring over old curios and offering them gifts can be one of the gentlest ways to broach the topic of your death.

But the death-cleaning ethos goes further than sorting through physical belongings. It's a clarion call to live life better by treasuring what makes you happy, rather than delaying dreaded tasks or amassing objects out of habit.

Opposite: It's a good idea to start death cleaning while you're still fit and healthy.

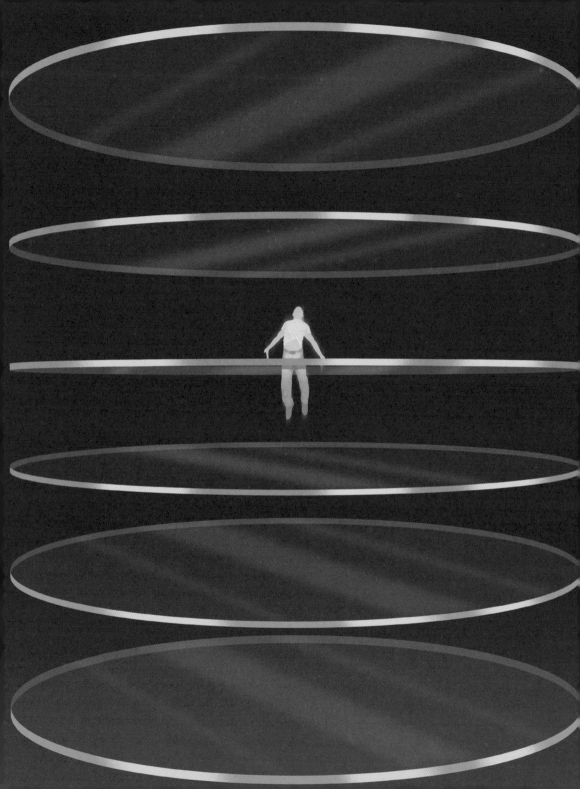

BUDDHISM'S SIXTH BARDO

Living and dying aren't opposites, and death isn't your final destination. To Buddhists, human existence cycles through six different states — and dying is just one phase along this cosmic journey.

" 'Y ou mustn't indulge in attachment to this life,' murmurs a soft voice. 'Do not cling to life."

These words from the *Bardo Thödol* (*Tibetan Book of the Dead*) are whispered into the ear of a newly dead person. With this encouragement, they are urged to renounce worldly attachments in order to pass between one life and the next.

Throughout the strands of Buddhism, death isn't seen as crossing an eternal threshold: it's a transition period in samsara, the cycle of birth and rebirth, where the only release is entering the state of moksha (enlightenment). These beliefs inform the common themes of Buddhist funerals, like vigils (often several days long), chanting (to help release the self from earthly life) and cremation (the Buddha was cremated).

RELEASED INTO THE NEXT LIFE
Otherwise, funeral customs can be as varied as the different Buddhist schools of thought. At Zen funerals, the deceased may be given a different name, to prevent them from returning if their earthly name is called. Theravada Buddhist communities crack open a coconut above the deceased, as a final cleansing. And though the practice is less common than it once was, some Tibetan Buddhists still dismember their dead and leave them at lofty open-air burial sites to be consumed by vultures (page 219), as a final act of generosity.

THE PROFOUND CALM OF ACCEPTANCE

As someone transitions through different bardo states, they let go of their ego and disconnect from passions and attachments. And as death approaches, it's even more important not to cling to life, to ensure a favourable rebirth. This acceptance offers the dying a path to approach death with less fear, but Buddhist death philosophy offers comfort for mourners, too. Death is not an ending, because every death is also a rebirth.

Hearing the news of a death can feel shocking, abrupt, even life-altering. At first, our minds and bodies reject the finality of this news; we might even enter denial, or plead with fate. But Buddhism encourages us to acknowledge a bardo, interval state, between death and the next phase of their journey. By murmuring words of encouragement to the dead, urging them to let go of their earthly attachments, we too are encouraged to let go.

THE SIX BARDOS

Tibetan Buddhists conceptualise human existence as cycling through six different interval states, or bardos. For those who have received Buddhist instruction, each of these states contains opportunities to experience the truth of reality and unlock them from the painful cycle of life, death and rebirth. Even death is a lesson in the truth of existence.

The first three bardos aren't consecutive; they're the different states a person can experience during their life. The first bardo is living, from birth until you draw your final breath. The second is dreaming, which challenges

Above: A Tibetan Buddhist monk holds prayer beads. Opposite: View of Swayambhunath, Kathmandu, one of Buddhism's holiest pilgrimage sites.

you not to succumb to dream-like illusions, nor to the illusory promises of living. The third is meditation, which Buddhists practise to cultivate clarity of thought, peacefulness and detachment from worldly things.

The next three bardos take you from one life into the next. The fourth bardo is when the body shows physical signs of death, at which point a lama may murmur lessons from the *Bardo Thödol* to guide them away from worldly desires – including the desire to hold on to life itself. The fifth is illumination, experienced only by those who have practised meditation enough to recognise the light of true nature. These deserving beings will experience a feeling of deep peace and crystal-clear awareness.

Then, finally, you reach the sixth bardo: transmigration of your essence into a new life. Depending on the karmic balance of your previous life, your soul may be drawn to a favourable rebirth, or into a life that takes you further from moksha. This 'bardo of becoming' is a hallucinatory state, moving between consciousness and unconsciousness for 49 days until the self hurtles to the next life.

GREEN BURIALS

Death is cruel, but it can also be kind – to the environment, that is. From water cremation to body composting, ecofriendly innovations are casting aside the wasteful burial practices of old.

In the US, most burials follow a rigid formula: the body is embalmed and placed inside a wooden casket, then lowered into a concrete-lined grave. But these legacy traditions have an enormous environmental cost: according to the Green Burial Council, more than 16.2 million litres (4.3 million gallons) of embalming fluid and 145 million kg (1.6 million tons) of concrete are used every year to embalm and bury the dead. Now, a backlash against these unsustainable traditions is underway: the US green burial movement seeks kinder ways to lay the dead to rest, and has inspired similar movements across Europe and Australia.

THE BIRTH OF THE DEATH INDUSTRY

There's no law in the US insisting that bodies must be buried in caskets. Embalming isn't legally required either, but roughly half of Americans choose it (the practice is exceedingly rare in Europe).

The rise of embalming in the US can be traced back to the Civil War, when bodies needed to be preserved for transportation across long distances. Embalming endured because it allowed more time to view and pay respects to a dead person before burial – without exposing the family to any perceptible signs of decay.

But what does a more sustainable funeral look like? At green burial sites, unembalmed bodies are wrapped in a silk shroud, or placed in a

BACK TO NATURE

Embalmers, particularly in the US, clean and prepare bodies to high cosmetic standards. They display the body in its best possible light and protect mourners from any signs of decay. But for many, it is unsettling to imagine our loved one being drained of their bodily fluids and injected with embalming fluid.

Green burials don't intervene in natural processes; they return a body to the earth unadorned. Rather than distancing mourners from the reality of death, green burials allow us to witness the finality of death in an intimate way: placing a body into the earth, or even sliding it into the waters of an aquamation tank. It can bring us solace to know that our loved one's body isn't invaded by harsh chemicals or handled by strangers.

There's also a moral consolation in knowing that our loved one's environmental beliefs and commitments are being upheld after death.

biodegradable coffin. At some burial grounds, like the Fernwood Cemetery in California, you can accelerate the decomposition process by being buried in a 'mushroom suit', a biodegradable shroud made from fungal spores that speed up the decomposition process, filtering away toxins that can contaminate the soil.

AT ONE WITH THE TREES

If a green burial site doesn't meet your expectations, you can spend the ever-after in a forest. Better

Place Forests allow you to pick a memorial tree in sites across the US. After death, your ashes are mixed with soil at the base of the tree, and wildflower seeds are sprinkled nearby.

You can also opt for burial inside a Capsula Mundi, a bioplastic container large enough to hold an entire body. In contrast with the incomplete decomposition that takes place when a body is buried in a solid casket, soil bacteria breaks down the Capsula Mundi, allowing

Above and opposite: Shrouds and coffins of wool felt; and coffins weaved from willow, bamboo and seagrass are among the possibilities for an environmentally gentle burial.

the remains to gradually come into contact with the soil; their nutrients can then be taken up by a tree above them.

Tree burial is also possible for people who choose cremation – but because of their high pH level, human ashes don't cultivate plant life without a little help. If you place ashes inside a Bios urn, the cremains are separated from seeds and seedlings for the first three months of their growth. This allows you to bury ashes and watch plantlife bloom in a forest, your garden or even a planter.

BODY COMPOSTING

If you want to truly optimise the nourishment your body gives back to the soil, choose body composting. Legal in six US states so far, including Washington, California and New York, the process uses carbon (for bacteria to consume) and nitrogen (to support bacterial growth) to break a body down to nutrient-rich soil.

Human composting startup Recompose, based in Seattle, offers the full service: first, there's a 'laying in' ceremony, which the family can attend.

Then the bacteria get to work. It takes between four and seven weeks to compost a body, before the soil – just under 1 cu metre (1 cu yd) per person – is given to the family, who may wish to use it in their gardens (or it can be donated to a nonprofit land trust). Overall, they claim, the process requires only an eighth of the energy of a traditional burial.

WATER CREMATION

Though cremations don't require as much land as burial, their environmental cost is steep: according to Chemical & Engineering News, each body can release almost 190kg (419lb) of carbon dioxide into the air – double the amount of a ground burial. A fire-free alternative is aquamation, where the body is placed inside a stainless steel container together with a water and alkali mix. It's heated up to rapidly deteriorate the body, leaving behind only bones, which can be broken down into ash to be kept in an urn, or scattered, by relatives and friends.

Though the process takes longer than cremation by fire, the temperature is lower and it consumes far less energy (up to 90% less fuel). For anyone who considers fire to be a harsh, consuming end, aquamation can feel like a gentler alternative: the liquid mixture simply acts as a catalyst to the natural process of decomposition that would happen over time. The technology is unfamiliar to most of us, but the theme remains the same: concluding the circle of life with gentleness and care to the dead, and to the planet.

Opposite: Inside a Recompose vessel, the body is transformed from human to soil in a nest of woodchips, alfalfa, and straw.

BODY DONATION: THE ULTIMATE GIFT

With green burials, your body can live on by nourishing the soil. But your body can also contribute to the good of humanity – if you donate it for scientific research.

The process is as simple as checking you qualify (if you're diagnosed with certain ongoing infectious diseases, you may not be eligible), and registering your donation with a university or teaching hospital. Ensure your next of kin are aware of your intentions, so they can act on these wishes immediately after you pass. Mentioning your donation in your will isn't enough, because it may not be read until days or weeks after your death.

After you donate your body, it will be used to train future medical practitioners or be part of research that can accelerate scientific breakthroughs, from cancer to heart disease. But while you may be given information about upcoming research programmes, you can't pick and choose your body's exact fate.

Body donation is also a thrifty option. Costs such as transporting the body and filing the death certificate are covered for you, and while your family won't have time to arrange a viewing of the body, your cremated remains will usually be returned after their scientific duties are complete.

CREMATION GHATS OF VARANASI

In India, death is supercharged with spirituality, much like life, and the journey to the next plane of existence takes place in full public view at the funeral ghats in Varanasi.

For devout Hindus, there is no greater honour than to die in sight of the River Ganges in Varanasi. This is Hinduism's most sacred city and the acrid smoke of funeral fires wafts along the banks of India's mother river, a constant reminder of Varanasi's position at the threshold between life and death.

The material and spiritual worlds have been flowing together in Varanasi since at least the second millennium BCE. Every year, more than 40,000

funerals take place at the ghats (ceremonial steps) on the banks of the Ganges, presided over by a caste of attendants whose entire lives are devoted to fuelling the funeral fires.

For Hindus, Varanasi is a place of intense emotion and profound spiritual power. For non-Hindus, the ghats are one of India's most moving and challenging spectacles – a visceral reminder of the ultimate destination of life in a world that prefers to keep mortality hidden from view.

A SACRED THRESHOLD

It's hard to imagine a more appropriate spot for the transition to the next life than Manikarnika Ghat, marking the spot where the earrings of Shiva's first wife, Sati, fell as her mourning husband carried her crumbling corpse across the Earth.

Dying in Varanasi is believed to be a direct route to moksha – release from the cycle of earthly rebirth into a state of perfection. As a preparation for paradise, it's akin to a Catholic receiving the last rites

PREPARING FOR MORTALITY

The lessons from Hindu cremation rituals are less about the physical disposal of the dead, and more about attitudes – to life, to dying, and to the relationship between the two. By incorporating acceptance of death into daily existence, Hinduism prepares its followers for the impermanence of earthly existence.

In Hinduism, as in Buddhism, contemplating the nature of mortality helps people focus on what is important about being alive: being compassionate, moral and virtuous, and treating others with respect. It doesn't make death painless, but it removes some of the anxiety.

Compare this to societies that avoid speaking about death, where the living are sheltered from the trauma of mortality, but also left unprepared for it. Death is life's one certainty, and hiding from it only amplifies the pain when people eventually encounter this unavoidable reality.

from the Pope on the steps of St Peter's Basilica in Rome.

Accordingly, many people in the final stages of life chose to spend their last days in the ashrams that line the banks of the Ganges, joined by a veritable army of sadhus (holy men) who live in a state of blessed simplicity during what they hope will be the final turn of the wheel of reincarnation.

"In Hinduism, there is a view that life is an act of preparation

Above and opposite: Funeral rites and rituals on the banks of the Ganges in Varanasi, Uttar Pradesh.

for a good death," explains Dr Ankur Barua, Senior Lecturer in Hindu Studies at the University of Cambridge. "At every moment, we are dying, and people try to absorb this process of change, decay and impermanence into the living fabric of their lives. It is the art of dying that helps us to live fully."

THE CYCLE OF LIFE

In Hindu philosophy, life and death are merely passing phases in the cycle of samsara (birth and rebirth). After death, the physical body is an empty vessel, and the dead are quickly cremated to free the soul to continue its journey.

"The true core of a human person is not the physical body,

Above: Dashashwamedh Ghat, known for the *ganga aarti* (holy fire ritual) that takes place at dusk every day.

but the imperishable self, which we call the atman or jiva," explains Dr Ankur Barua. "Life is regarded as an ongoing moral progression, where each lifetime represents a chance to purify ourselves. If we fail to complete this process in one lifetime, the funeral rituals help the immaterial soul move to a new embodiment."

To prepare for cremation, the body is washed with ghee, honey, yoghurt and milk and wrapped in a white shroud with a garland of lotus flowers – symbolising rebirth from adversity – then transported to the funeral grounds, usually within 24 hours of death.

Cremations are held in full public view, allowing everyone present to see that the divine part of the person has departed this world. Hymns are chanted, wood smoke swirls, and sacred cows wander idly between the pyres, yet the crowds of mourners maintain a remarkably matter-of-fact attitude towards the charring human remains.

VARANASI'S DEATH-KEEPERS

The production line of cremations at Varanasi involves logistics on an industrial scale. Vast loads of firewood are delivered daily to dealers behind the funeral

ghats – sandalwood for the wealthy, common timbers for less prosperous families – alongside strips of bamboo that are lashed together to make funeral biers.

For the Doms of Varanasi – caretakers of the city's funeral fires – ushering the deceased into the next life is a job they were born into, and a profession they will pass onto their children. Although they play a vital role at the end of life, the city's 300 or so funeral attendants are Dalits, or 'untouchables' – forbidden from coming into physical contact with members of other castes except in death.

GREENING VARANASI'S FUNERALS

Once, the wood for Varanasi's funeral pyres was gathered from the eastern banks of the Ganges, but the shore is now denuded of trees as far as the eye can see. It is estimated that funeral ghats burn through 72,575kg (80 tons) of firewood every day, releasing 1.8 billion kg (2 million tons) of carbon dioxide into the atmosphere. And the disposal of huge quantities of ashes has contributed to

transforming the Ganges into India's most polluted river.

But change is coming. The Indian government is involved in an ambitious programme to reduce the flow of industrial and agricultural waste, sewage and human ashes into the river. Meanwhile, independent charities have opened special *asthi kalash* (funeral urn) banks, where relatives can store ashes for the prescribed mourning period, after which time they can be buried on land.

Simultaneously, new 'greenatoriums' combining elements of traditional funerals and electric cremations are coming, reducing the carbon footprint of Varanasi's funeral industry. However, environmentalists are urging faster action – in 2022, the Ganges burst its banks, forcing mourners to stage cremations on terraces and in the streets, giving new urgency to attempts to green Varanasi's funeral ghats.

After the body has been totally consumed by the flames, attendants hand over the ashes to the family to be scattered on moving water – usually the murky waters of the Ganges – to aid the movement of the soul to the next existence. It's a ritual as old as India itself, and a powerful reminder of India's ongoing belief in the cycle of life.

Right: A ritual farewell for the soul of the deceased. Opposite: Wood piles for cremations at Manikarnika Ghat.

SEE IT FOR YOURSELF

Visiting Manikarnika Ghat is a profoundly affecting experience, but it must be done respectfully. The funeral ghats lie within strolling distance of Varanasi's main traveller hub in the Old City, but you can't just wander between cremation plinths. Instead, you'll be led by priests to a raised viewing area behind the ghats, where you can observe – but not photograph – the pyres.

Visitors to the viewing deck are expected to make a sizeable donation towards the running costs of the cremations. If you prefer a less transactional experience, view the ghats from the river. Boats are available for hire at many of the ghats lining the eastern shore of the Ganges, and boat guides meander slowly along the eastern riverbank, passing close to Manikarnika and other ceremonial sites.

As part of a Ganges boat trip, you'll pass ghats used for other important Hindu rituals, such as the *Ganga aarti* fire ceremony, which takes place in the early evening at Dashashwamedh Ghat to honour the sacred river. Once upon a time, Gangetic dolphins frequented this stretch of river, but these days, you'll have to travel north to the confluence with the Gomti River for reliable sightings.

JAINISM'S GENTLE ART OF DYING

According to Jainism, even your death can be a dutiful act of care. This ancient religion upholds nonviolence as its ultimate principle – inspiring gentle, ecofriendly funeral ceremonies.

Fragrant smoke curls from incense sticks, and chanting sets a pensive mood – but at this funeral, there won't be flowers. Jainism practitioners depart from this life in the same humble way they lived.

Only a tiny minority of Indians today are Jains, but the religion of Jain Dharma, or Jainism, is one of the world's oldest faiths. Like Hindus, Jains aim to free themselves from samsara (the painful cycle of birth and rebirth) to reach the state of moksha:

enlightenment and release.

To achieve moksha, Jains follow principles of nonviolence, nonabsolutism and nonattachment to possessions. But ahimsa (nonviolence) is the greatest of all duties; without it, other practices barely tip the karmic scale. Ahimsa encompasses non-harm to any life form – human, animal or insect – whether committed deliberately or not. Accordingly, Jainist last rites (Antim Sanskar) also uphold nonviolence and asceticism.

CLEANSING AND CREMATION

A dying person may limit their diet to rice and water in an act of heightened self-discipline. Shortly after death, the family will wash the body and dress the deceased in white, placing a swastika (an ancient symbol of wellbeing in Jainism and Hinduism) nearby. Incense is lit, bhajan (devotional song) is chanted for up to an hour, and a family member utters a personal eulogy.

Next, the body is prepared for cremation with three sprinklings

LETTING GO IS HARD TO DO

Death and life in Jainism are frugal. Funerals are unadorned, and some Jains gradually cast off earthly comforts as death draws near – in the most extreme cases, with a 'final fast'.

Letting go is hard to do, but to Jains, giving up our attachments helps usher our souls toward their greater purpose: the state of moksha. To nonbelievers, this purposefulness and self-control is an astonishing way to approach death – and worlds away from being fearfully resigned to our fate.

Intentionally discarding the vestiges of our earthly lives is a way of accepting the inevitable. It returns our agency. Jains focus less on what is lost when a life ends, and more on the spiritual goal of moksha.

In Jainism, this life is just a waypoint on a longer journey. But whatever our faith, it's humbling to accept that our lives and deaths are mere specks in the universe's vast drama.

of water and rice, along with ghee and fragrant sandalwood. Cremation takes place during the day and as soon after death as possible. The area is meticulously cleared to ensure that even small insects are not caught up in the funeral pyre.

A family member, usually the eldest son, circumambulates the cremation site three times while chanting the *Namōkāra mantra*, the most significant of all Jain prayers: a reminder of the ultimate goal of moksha.

As for the ashes, they will be dispersed with exceptional care, ensuring they don't pollute rivers or harm wildlife.

INSTANT REBIRTH
Death is a step along the path to eventually achieving moksha. For this reason, Jain families grieve

Above: Jain nuns in mourning. Opposite: Pilgrims worshipping at the Gommateshwara statue dedicated to Bahubali, a symbol of Jain precepts of peace, nonviolence, sacrifice of worldly affairs, and simple living.

modestly, focusing on meditation rather than mourning.

That's not to say that Jains condemn mourning; this would be a kind of violence. But mourning is attachment to something already passed, because rebirth is believed to take place immediately after death.

THE 'FINAL FAST'

Considering the principle of non-harm, it's striking that Jainism has a rare death custom that seems almost inconceivable to outsiders: the 'final fast', or *sallekhana* (literally, 'thinning out').

Only committed by nuns, monks or highly devout people, *sallekhana* is the ultimate renunciation of earthly life. Practitioners spend their time in prayer and gradually reduce their consumption of food and drink. This is believed to reduce negative karma, which affects a soul's rebirth into future lives.

If you're unsettled by the idea of self-imposed starvation, you aren't alone. First, the High Court of Rajasthan banned the practice, though this was overturned by India's Supreme Court. *Sallekhana* is extreme; although it may seem shocking to modern western sensibilities, it's a remarkable act of self-determination and fearlessness in the face of death.

HANGING COFFINS OF SAGADA

In the mountain village of Sagada, the dead watch over the living from a lofty perch. Coffins are strung high on cliffs in a custom that has lasted for millennia.

The karst cliffs of the Philippines are remote and forbidding, instantly inspiring awe. They might also be the most spectacular burial location on Earth.

In Sagada, among the imposing mountains of the Philippines' largest island, nature is arranged vertically. Bone-white limestone cliffs rise dramatically above the treeline. Clinging to these cliffs are gravity-defying molave trees, which burst forth from pockets of soil. These sheer walls of limestone are regularly pockmarked with caves where bats roost, while lizards snooze in the narrowest fissures.

Look closer and you'll see coffins fastened to the cliff face, high above the ground. Known as 'hanging coffins', many are painted with bold lettering to indicate the names of their inhabitants. They're balanced on wooden brackets that have been jimmied into the cliff face, or placed on rocky overhangs or within caves.

SEATED IN THE DEATH CHAIR

The region's Igorot people have practised cliff burials for more than 2000 years, and many of the coffins you can see today are centuries old. Hanging coffins are much less common than they once were, and when the tradition continues, it's reserved for community leaders (most of them men) – the higher the coffin, the higher its inhabitant's status.

Before death, an elderly person carves their own coffin (enlisting family and friends to

A SAFE PLACE TO REST

Numerous Asian cultures have strung their coffins high. Like the Philippines' Igorot people, the Toraja people of Sulawesi, Indonesia, also hang coffins from cliffs and secret them away in caves. Hanging coffins were once customary in parts of China's Yunnan and Sichuan provinces, mostly among the Bo people; it's thought they wanted to lay their dead somewhere inaccessible, so that bodies were not disturbed.

In communities that faced the threat of headhunters desecrating graves, hanging coffins were a practical measure. But the desire to keep our loved ones safe, even in death, is a natural extension of the protectiveness we feel while they are alive. Cliff burials keep our dear departed out of harm's way, allowing us to safeguard those we love. But cliff burials also keep them within sight, helping us to accept their new state; it's a healthy balance between acceptance and continued acts of care.

help, if they're unable to do so). When they pass away, their family places their body in a wooden *sangadil* (death chair) and cloaks them in a blanket, before smoking the body to preserve it. Relatives arrive to pay their last respects, before the body is placed inside the coffin.

In the past, it was common to break the deceased's bones, in order to fold them into a small coffin, with their knees tucked beneath their chin. In this way, their life could end the same way it began: in the foetal position. Nowadays, increasing squeamishness about breaking

Above: Around 100 coffins are stacked at the entrance of Sagada's Lumiang Burial Cave. Opposite: Rice terraces in Ifugao province, northern Philippines.

the bones of the dead has created a growing demand for longer coffins.

CLOSER TO HEAVEN

According to folklore, the deads' vitality and intelligence can be transmitted through fluids that emanate from the corpse. During the procession to the cliff-burial site, mourners might try to touch the dearly departed in order to absorb their essence.

Finally, the coffin is carefully hoisted up the cliff face and balanced on a rocky outcrop or atop wooden brackets. At this lofty height, the dead are considered to be closer to the spirits of their ancestors. (But yes, the coffins do sometimes fall, especially if the wood deteriorates over time.)

The proceedings conclude with a huge funeral feast, where chickens and pigs are sacrificed, three or five animals at a time.

In this region of waterfalls, low-hanging mists and vivid green ricefields, Sagada's hanging coffins have become a tourist curiosity. You can visit the most famous site (ideally with a local guide): Lumiang Burial Cave, where more than 100 coffins are stacked into a forbidding wall. Echo Valley is another nearby location.

TIBETAN SKY BURIALS

High in the mountains of Tibet, the dead perform a final act of grace: offering their own bodies to vultures.

A lone vulture wheels above Tibet's Zhorong-chu Valley, circling a plateau where burial attendants have laid an offering on the ground. When the vulture finally lands, dozens more take this as their cue: they swoop down and swarm the offering, forming a pulsating carpet of dark-brown feathers. Once their hunger is sated, the birds return to the sky one by one, leaving behind nothing but human bones.

This is a sky burial, also known as *jhator* (giving alms to birds). Offering the remains of the dead to vultures is a custom that endures in remote parts of Tibet, like the sacred charnel house at the 12th-century Drigung Til Monastery. The tradition has endured for more than 11,000 years – for both spiritual and geographic reasons.

RITUAL PREPARATIONS

According to the *Bardo Thödol* (commonly known as the *Tibetan Book of the Dead*), an individual passes through transitional states in between their births, deaths and rebirths. Tibetan death customs aim to guide their path, and ensure that they aren't pulled into a lesser rebirth.

The day before a sky burial, the body is prepared amid burning incense and ceremonial chants. Hair and nails might be clipped and given to the family. The body is wrapped in linen and may be laid on a ritual throne overnight, which is believed to guarantee a human rebirth in the next life.

FINAL ACT OF GRACE

In a sky burial, the remnants of an earthly life are offered up to nature as a gift. Not only does this uphold compassion, a tenet of Buddhism's path to liberation from samsara (the cycle of death and rebirth), it's a powerful act of comfort and hope. The deceased's life ends with an act of grace that forever connects them to nature's cycle of renewal. Sky burials can offer closure in a curiously poetic way: nothing remains but winged ambassadors, who soar up to the clouds.

It's also an alternative to burial rituals that preserve the body's physicality, like embalming, which can be disquieting and prolong mourners' distress. After all, it's traumatic to see a loved one lifeless – but Tibetan Buddhism consoles us that their remains are not them. This delineation between the living self and the dead body encourages us to remember the deceased with all their former vitality.

GIVEN OVER TO NATURE

Some Tibetans travel from miles around to auspicious sky burial sites like Drigung Til Monastery. But although this custom is deemed an honourable end-of-life ritual in Tibet, those unfamiliar with sky burials might wince initially upon learning the details.

On the day of the sky burial, the body is carried up to the site and laid on a flat stone. It is prepared for the vultures with exacting cuts from the knife of a *rogyapa* (burial attendant, literally 'one who breaks bodies'). Then come the vultures, either of their own accord or summoned by the

Above: Vultures gather at Drigung Thil Monastery in Lhasa. Opposite top: Inside Drigung Thil. Bottom: Lhasa's Potala Palace, former residence of the Dalai Lama and pilgrimage site for Tibetan Buddhists.

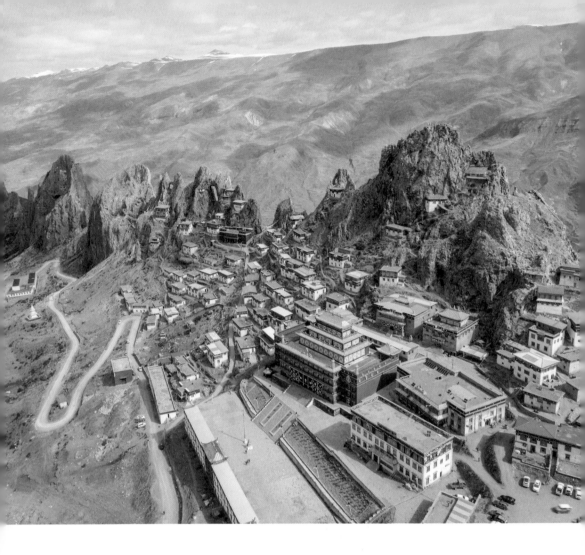

burial attendants. Their raspy cries fill the air as they swarm the body in a feeding frenzy.

The deceased's loved ones may watch from a discreet distance away. Meanwhile, monks may observe the number of vultures that descend onto the body: if the body attracts multitudes of birds, this is thought to reflect an accumulation of good karma during a lifetime. If there are few birds, or if the vultures refuse to feed altogether, the opposite is true.

Usually, it only takes a matter of minutes for vultures to pick the bones clean. The *rogyapa* returns with a mallet to grind up the bones, mixing them with barley and yak butter before scattering them to feed smaller animals.

AN ANCIENT, ECOFRIENDLY PRACTICE

Sky burials stem from a belief that at the instant of death the human soul moves on. The body left behind contains nothing of the essence of what made the person human, and offering the body to vultures to feed on is a pure act of karmic grace.

Considering Tibet's climate, sky burials are also immensely practical. Tibet's people were historically nomads, and as they navigated harsh terrain, they made thrifty use of every available resource. Cremating the dead with precious fuel would be a waste, while burial of bodies would be impossible in a climate where the ground freezes iron-hard. After all, burial in the ground also submits a body to natural decomposition. Sky burials are simply a different ritual for offering a body to nature.

Sky burials act as reminders of Buddhist teachings. In Buddhism, the earthly realm is characterised by impermanence, so it's fitting that every last remainder of a person is consumed or scattered.

SACRED SKY SPIRITS

Animist belief systems intermingle with sky burial traditions. Many ancient Tibetans attributed spiritual qualities to animals, including vultures, which were considered spirits of the sky. Today, some Tibetans think of them as *dākinī*, feminine spirits with the power to ritually consume humans. To anyone accustomed to thinking of vultures as eerie carrion eaters, this provides a new lens to view them through: disposing of remains ceases to be taboo, and is instead endowed with a sacred importance.

And of course, death is not the end. As the *Tibetan Book of the Dead* explains, existence is a cycle of birth, suffering, death and rebirth, which we can only escape through spiritual enlightenment. By allowing the deceased a final act of good karma, their loved ones hope to take them one step closer to freedom from this cycle.

Opposite: Zizhu Temple, Dingqing, Tibet, was built 3000 years ago.

TABOO TOURISM

After years of provisional rulings to ban tourists from attending sky burials, in 2015 Tibet finally passed a bill to protect sky burials from sightseers and photographers. Not only was this a move to guard an ancient cultural practice from prying eyes, it aimed to end an industry that was crafting an uncomfortable narrative that 'otherised' Tibetan people, showcasing their traditions as brutal or backward. Other laws protect humans and vultures alike; for example, sky burials of people who died of contagious illnesses are forbidden.

Despite the tourist ban, some Tibetan guides continue to facilitate visits to sky burial sites. With such a visceral spectacle, it's challenging for even the most careful guides to ensure their visitors behave appropriately at burial sites – especially when some tourists arrive in search of social media 'likes', rather than cultural edification. Instead of seeking out a sky burial, contemplate the cycle of death and rebirth at several sites in Lhasa. The formidable Tomb of Tsongkhapa, which houses the skull fragments of the legendary philosopher-monk, is a popular pilgrimage place. Or, visit Potala Palace to gaze up at the burial stupas of Dalai Lamas past.

REMEMBERED IN STONE
The World's Most Impressive Tombs

Constructed by armies of workers, stunning in scale and often shrouded in mystery, the grandiose tombs of the past demonstrate the eternal importance of a fitting sendoff.

Throughout history, we have lovingly constructed homes for the dead. Inscriptions from diverse ancient civilisations — in Mesopotamia, China, Greece, Mesoamerica — stress the importance of respectful burial and the dire consequences of neglecting to do so. Almost universally, this respect included provisions for a life after death. Even in prehistoric times, people were buried with 'grave goods' — articles necessary for navigating the afterlife and gifts for offering to the keepers of the underworld.

By the time Ancient Egyptians built the pyramids, perhaps the world's most famous tombs, their purpose had expanded. Now, the tomb was also a monument to the memory of the dead — the more important the departed, the more impressive the structure. But unanswered questions surrounding the construction and exact function of extraordinary mausoleums like the Giza pyramids and Europe's Neolithic passage tombs expose the mysteries at the heart of these ancient belief systems. These are also monuments to the ultimate unknowability of the past.

One of the 8000 terracotta warriors that protect the spirit of Emperor Qin Shi Huang.

China's Terracotta Army

The famous soldiers of the Terracotta Army are no idle stand-abouts. Their purpose is clear: they are here to guard over Qin Shi Huang, China's first emperor, in the afterlife. The 8000-odd life-sized warrior figures were buried with the emperor in 210–209 BCE as part of sprawling necropolis thought to spread over 92 sq km (38 sq miles). Accompanying the warriors are over 130 terracotta chariots and 600-plus horses as well as nonmilitary figures: officials, acrobats, strongmen and musicians. Each figure has individual facial features and was originally painted with coloured lacquers and ground precious stones — what's thought to be the work of 700,000 workers over nearly three decades.

Emperor Qin's tomb itself remains a hermetically sealed mystery. Ancient accounts tell of mercury streams inlaid in its floor; earth samples tested highly positive for mercury in 2005. Debate continues over whether to attempt an excavation, and how to best protect both its contents and workers at the site.

Above: Soldiers of the Terracotta Army.

Great Pyramid of Giza, Egypt

The Great Pyramid is the only one of the Seven Wonders of the Ancient World still standing. The oldest and tallest of the three main Giza pyramids, it was built around 2550 BCE by Pharaoh Khufu (Khafre and Menkaure followed later with their slightly humbler efforts). Towering 146m (479ft) when first built, the ravages of time have reduced its height to 138m (453ft); its estimated 2.3 million stone blocks each weigh up to 72,575kg (80 tons). Along with its smaller cousins, it would originally have had an outer casing of white limestone, making an even more dazzling spectacle, gleaming in the desert sun.

The little open space inside its hulking mass is austerely lined with granite blocks (lavishly decorated, treasure-packed burial chambers like Tutankhamen's would come later). A small subterranean burial chamber lies beneath. Historians theorise that the pyramid form may represent a stairway for the pharaoh's soul to reach the heavens — but its true meaning, and the secrets of its construction, remain a mystery.

Above: The Giza Pyramids at sunset.

Shah-i-Zinda, Uzbekistan

This remarkable complex in Samarkand is perhaps the world's oldest and longest-running construction site. Gradually expanded over eight centuries (the 11th until the 19th), the 'street of the dead' counts over 20 buildings, tombs for both the famed and the unknown. During the 14th and 15th centuries it was an architectural testing ground, producing some of the Muslim world's richest mosaic work in a harmonious spectacle of sparkling blue and green tiles.

Its name, meaning 'Tomb of the Living King', refers to its original, innermost and holiest shrine – the cool, quiet rooms around the resting place of Qusam ibn-Abbas, a cousin of the Prophet Muhammad who is said to have brought Islam here in the 7th century. Legend has it that he is not in fact dead, but descended into a well and remains the king of an underground paradise. Certainly, his memory endures here, in an age-old necropolis that has survived and bloomed through centuries of war, weather and progress.

The stunning tilework of Shah-i-Zinda.

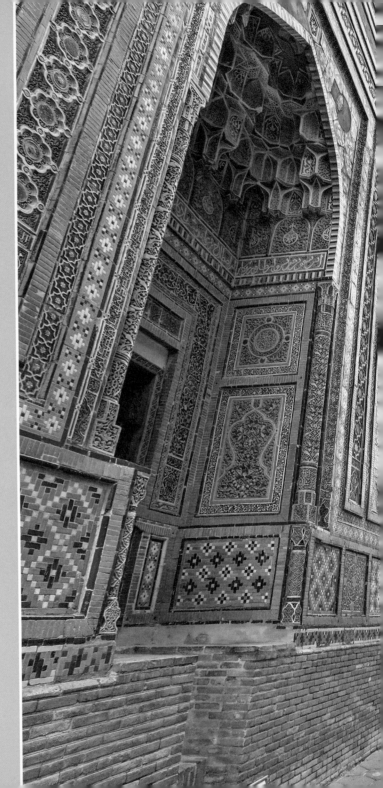

India's Taj Mahal

A shrine to love, a marvel of architectural harmony, one of the world's most instantly recognisable buildings – it's all these things, but the Taj Mahal is also a colossal tomb. Built by Mughal emperor Shah Jahan to immortalise his wife Mumtaz Mahal after she died in childbirth in 1631, the Taj draws millions each year to its home in the northern Indian state of Agra. At the centre of a complex including a mosque and paradisical gardens, the mausoleum is made of a white marble that constantly changes hue – pale pink at sunrise, dazzling white at high noon, translucent blue at night.

Tradition says that Shah Jahan originally intended to build a mirror mausoleum in black marble across the river for his own remains. Instead he lies here, alongside his beloved wife – not in the mausoleum's grand cenotaphs surrounded by carvings and semiprecious stones, but in a quiet garden-level room below.

Newgrange, Ireland

Centuries before the appearance of Stonehenge or the pyramids of Giza, a thriving Stone Age community constructed an exceptional example of what today's archaeologists classify as a passage tomb. Draped across the rich farmlands of Ireland's Boyne Valley, the circular mound – 85m (279ft) in diameter and 13m (43ft) high – is filled with passageways and chambers, and is surrounded by 97 intricately engraved kerbstones.

Its exact purpose is a mystery. The exhumation of human bones (both burnt and unburnt) points to a ritual funerary function, but it's thought to have held a wider significance to its Neolithic builders, connected to astrological knowledge and ancestor worship. Mythical heroes and kings were said to be buried here; in Irish tradition it was the home of the Dagda, the chief of the Tuatha Dé Danann, a race of supernatural beings said to have inhabited ancient Ireland. The Newgrange burial mound is said to be an entrance to their realm, the Otherworld.

Left: The Taj Mahal, reflected. Above: Stone Age Newgrange.

INDEX

By chuckling at a WRY EPITAPH, we're sharing A JOKE WITH THE DEAD

INDEX

Guide to Death, Grief and Rebirth
July 2024
Published by Lonely Planet Global Limited
CRN 554153
www.lonelyplanet.com
10 9 8 7 6 5 4 3 2 1
Printed in Malaysia
ISBN 978 18375 8005 7
© Lonely Planet 2024
© photographers as indicated 2024

Publishing Director Piers Pickard
Illustrated & Gift Publisher Becca Hunt
Senior Editor Robin Barton
Editors Janine Eberle, Polly Thomas
Senior Designer Emily Dubin
Cover Design Dan Di Paolo
Layout Design Jo Dovey
Illustrator Avinash Weerasekera
Picture Research Ceri James
Print Production Nigel Longuet

Written by Anita Isalska with Joe Bindloss

Illustrations: © Avinash Weerasekera
Cover photograph: © David Cabrera Navarro | Alamy Stock Photo

STAY IN TOUCH lonelyplanet.com/contact
Lonely Planet Global Limited
Digital Depot, Roe Lane (off Thomas St),
Digital Hub, Dublin 8, D08 TCV4
IRELAND